Alchemy and Kabbalah in the Tarot

DETAIL FROM JOSHUA PASSING THE RIVER JORDAN WITH THE ARK [IE.
ARCANUM] OF THE COVENANT, BY BENJAMIN WEST (1800)

"And there I [יהוה] will meet with thee, and I will speak with thee
from above the ark-cover, from between the two cherubim which
are upon the ark of the testimony..." —Shemot / Exodus 25

"Rabbi Katina said, 'When the Israelites would ascend [to the
Holy Temple] on the festival, [the priest/kohen] would roll up the
curtain for them, and display for them the cherubim, who were joined
together [in an embrace]...' Rabba bar Rav Shila explains that "[The
cherubim appeared in the engravings] as a man joined in an embrace
with his female companion." —Babylonian Talmud, Yoma 54a

"Said Resh Lakish, 'When the Gentiles entered the sanctuary, they saw (the
engravings of) the cherubim joined together in an embrace. They took (the
engravings) out to the marketplace, and they said, Should these Israelites...
be involved in such (erotic) matters? Immediately, (the Romans) debased
(the Israelites), as it is said, (Lamentations 1:8) All who once respected her
(Israel), debased her, for they saw her nakedness.'" —Talmud, Yoma 54b

ALCHEMY AND KABBALAH IN THE TAROT

SAMAEL AUN WEOR

GLORIAN

Alchemy and Kabbalah in the Tarot

A Glorian Book / 2021

Originally published in Spanish as "Curso Esoterico de Kabala" (1969).

This Edition © 2021 Glorian Publishing

Print ISBN: 978-1-943358-16-8

Ebook ISBN: 978-1-934206-80-5

Glorian Publishing is a non-profit organization. All proceeds go to further the distribution of these books. For more information, visit glorian.org.

Contents

Illustrations

The Kabbalah is the science of numbers.

The author of the Tarot was the Angel Metatron. He is a lord of the serpent wisdom. The Bible refers to him as the Prophet Enoch.

The Angel Metatron, or Enoch, delivered the Tarot, in which the entirety of divine wisdom is enclosed. The Tarot remains written in stone.

He also left us the twenty-two letters of the Hebrew alphabet.

This great master lives in the superior worlds, in the world of Atziluth, which is a world of indescribable happiness. According to the Kabbalah, this world is the region of Kether, a very high sephirah.

All Kabbalists base themselves on the Tarot, and it is necessary for them to comprehend the Tarot and study it deeply.

The universe was made with the laws of numbers, measurements, and weight. Mathematics forms the universe, and the numbers become living entities.

—Samael Aun Weor, *Tarot and Kabbalah*

Editor's Introduction

To aid your study of this profound book, we have included a short glossary of terms at the end. You can find a much more detailed glossary at glorian.org.

Mantra Pronunciation

In this book the author provides mantras for our benefit. Chanting or repetition of sacred sounds is universal in all religions. In Sanskrit, these sounds are called mantras, and their repetition is called japa.

Generally speaking, the sounds in mantras are pronounced using the ancient roots (Latin, Greek, Hebrew, Sanskrit, etc):

I: as the ee in "tree"

E: as the eh in "they"

O: as the oh in "holy"

U: as the u in "true"

A: as the ah in "father"

M: extended as if humming, "mmmmm"

S: extended like a hiss, "sssss"

CH: if the word is Latin, pronounced as k. If the word is Hebrew, pronounced as a scrape in the back of the throat, as in "Bach"

G: In most mantras, G is pronounced as in "give"

Should Mantras be Spoken Aloud or Silent?

"...the verb is of triple pronunciation and that it endows three norms: verbal, mental, and conscious. One can articulate with the creative larynx, one can vocalize with his thought, and one can vocalize with the superlative consciousness of the Being." –Samael Aun Weor, *Esoteric Medicine and Practical Magic*

"There are three ways that one learns to use a mantra, to repeat prayers or sounds. They are quite simple: aloud, quietly, or silently.

Vaikhari Japa: verbal, loud

Upamshu Japa: whispered or hummed

Manasika Japa: mental, silent, without moving."
–the lecture Yoga of Devotion

"The fruits of whispered japa are a thousand times more powerful than the verbal japa, and the fruits of the silent, mental japa are hundreds of thousands of times more powerful than the verbal japa. Mental japa can even be kept up while at work." –Swami Sivananda

Preface

Beloved and immortal beings,
Greetings and adorations,
Beloved disciples,
There are two types of kabbalists: intellectual kabbalists and intuitive kabbalists. The intellectual kabbalists are black magicians, whilst the intuitive kabbalists are white magicians.

Many times the sidereal gods answer our questions by showing us a Tarot card; we must intuitively comprehend the answer that is given onto us. Intuitive kabbalists comprehend what destiny held in reserve to them by just seeing any card of the Tarot.

Gnostic Kabbalah is the doctrine of practical Christification. We do not theorize here. This is a one hundred percent practical work. Many students long for their Christification but they do not know where to start, because they do not know the clue, the secret.

Here we give away the clue, the secret, the key, to every student. Here is the clue, thirsty lovers of the truth: now practice.

You are not alone. We love you profoundly, thus when you tread on the path of the razor's edge, you will be internally assisted by the brothers and sisters of the temple.

In this course we deliver the clue of resurrection.[1] We have torn the veil of the sanctuary. Here you have all the secrets; here are all the clues of Christification. Here is written the doctrine that the Beloved taught in secret to his humble disciples.

The Beloved One will remain with us until the end of times. This is his doctrine. Here you have it: study it and practice it.

---

1   To rise again after death.

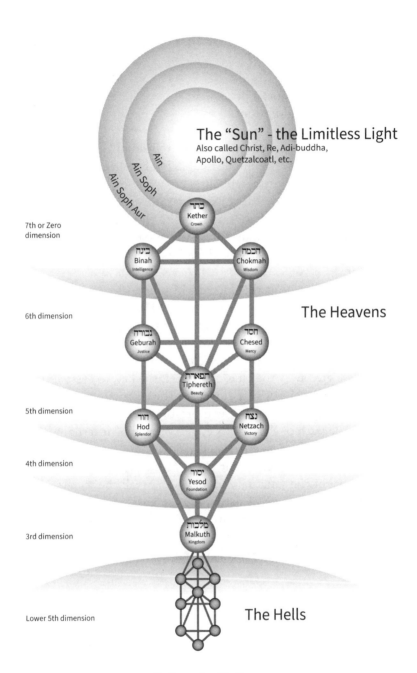

The "Sun" - the Limitless Light
Also called Christ, Re, Adi-buddha, Apollo, Quetzalcoatl, etc.

Ain
Ain Soph
Ain Soph Aur

7th or Zero dimension

כתר
Kether
Crown

בינה
Binah
Intelligence

חכמה
Chokmah
Wisdom

6th dimension

The Heavens

גבורה
Geburah
Justice

חסד
Chesed
Mercy

תפארת
Tiphereth
Beauty

5th dimension

הוד
Hod
Splendor

נצח
Netzach
Victory

4th dimension

יסוד
Yesod
Foundation

3rd dimension

מלכות
Malkuth
Kingdom

Lower 5th dimension

The Hells

THE TREE OF LIFE: THE KABBALAH

Introduction

Children of man, do you want to enter into the ineffable joy of nirvana?[2]

Do you want to become as gods?

Do you want to convert yourselves into Christs?

Do you want to liberate yourselves from the wheel of birth and death?

Here we will give you the clue of sexual magic![3] What else do you want?

Let us start by observing the relationship between the ten sephiroth[4] and the first ten cards of the Tarot.

The seven planets[5] of the solar system are the seven sephiroth, and the thrice-spiritual Sun[6] is the sephirothic crown.

These sephiroth live and palpitate within our consciousness, and we must learn to manipulate and combine them in the marvelous laboratory of our interior universe.

The ten sephiroth are:

Kether כתר, "crown"; the equilibrated power; the magician, the First Arcanum of the Tarot whose primeval hieroglyph is represented by a man.

Chokmah חכמה, "wisdom"; the Popess of the Tarot; esoteric wisdom, the Priestess. The second card of the Tarot; the moon; the primeval hieroglyph is represented by the mouth of man.

---

2 (Sanskrit) Literally, "cessation," referring to the ending of repeated cycles of suffering (samsara).

3 See glossary.

4 (Hebrew) The "Sefirot" (סְפִירוֹת), singular "Sefirah" (סְפִירָה), from ספר ("to count") literally means "counting" or "enumeration", yet also sefer (text), sippur (recounting a story), sappir (sapphire, brilliance, luminary). A sephirah is a symbol used in Kabbalah to represent levels of manifestation ranging from the very subtle to the very dense.

5 In esotericism, the seven planets represent the law of seven, which organizes manifested nature. This does not imply that there are only seven planets in our solar system.

6 The law of three, as represented by the solar trinities of all religions.

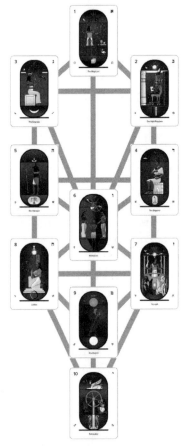

TAROT AND THE TREE OF LIFE

Binah בינה, "intelligence"; the planet Venus; third card
of the Tarot, the Empress, primeval hieroglyph is
represented by a hand in the attitude of grasping.

These three sephiroth are the Sephirothic Crown.

The seven inferior sephiroth come in the following order:

Chesed חסד, "mercy"; Jupiter, the Divine Being, Atman,
whose primeval hieroglyph is represented by a breast.
The fourth card of the Tarot, the Emperor.

Geburah גבורה, "severity"; the buddhic body of the human being, the Pope or the Hierophant of the Tarot, Mars, the warrior of Aries.

Tiphereth תפארת, "beauty," Venus of Taurus, love of the Holy Spirit, the causal body of the human being, the sixth card of the Tarot, the Lover.

Netzach נצח, "victory," Justice of the arcana, the seventh card of the Tarot, the chariot, Saturn.

Hod הוד, "glory," Mercury of Gemini, the eighth card of the Tarot, the Eternity of all.

Yesod יסוד, "foundation," the Sun of Leo, the ninth card of the Tarot. The Hermit, the Absolute.

Malkuth מלכות, "kingdom," the entire universe, Mary or Virgo, Nature.

These ten sephiroth live within our Being and are our inner solar system.

The Tarot is intimately related with esoteric astrology and with initiation.

Arcanum 10: First hour of Apollonius. Transcendental study of esotericism.

Arcanum 11: Second hour of Apollonius. Strength; the abysses of fire; the astral virtues form a circle through the dragons and fire. Study of the hidden forces.

Arcanum 12: Third hour of Apollonius. The serpents, the dogs and the fire; sexual alchemy; Sexual Magic, work with the Kundalini.[7]

Arcanum 13: Fourth hour of Apollonius. The neophyte will wander at night among the sepulchers, will experience the horror of visions, and will be submitted to magic and goethia; this means that the disciple will be aware that he is being attacked by millions of black magicians within the astral plane;[8] these tenebrous

---

7 See glossary.
8 The emotional aspect of the fifth dimension, where we dream, which in Kabbalah is related to the sephirah Hod.

magicians attempt to drive the disciple away from the luminous path.

Arcanum 14: Fifth hour of Apollonius. The two amphorae: divine and human magnetism; the superior waters of heaven. During this time the disciple learns to be pure and chaste because one comprehends the value of one's seminal liquor.

Arcanum 15: Sixth hour of Apollonius. The electric hurricane, Typhon Baphomet. Here it is necessary to remain quiet, still, due to fear; this signifies the terrible ordeal of the Guardian of the Threshold,[9] before whom a lot of courage is needed in order to overcome him.

Arcanum 16: Seventh hour of Apollonius. The fire comforts inanimate beings, and if any priest, a sufficiently purified man, steals the fire and then projects it, if he mixes this fire with sacred oil and consecrates it, then he will achieve the healing of all sicknesses by simply applying it to the afflicted areas. Here the initiate becomes aware that one's material wealth is threatened and one's business fails.

Arcanum 17: Eighth hour of Apollonius. The star of hope. The star of the Magi; the astral virtues of the elements, of the seeds of every genre.

Arcanum 18: Ninth hour of Apollonius. Study of the Minor Mysteries,[10] the nine arcades on which the student must ascend.

Arcanum 19: Tenth hour of Apollonius. The resplendent light. The doors of heaven open and one comes out of one's lethargy. This is the number ten of the second great Initiation of Major Mysteries[11] that allows the initiate to travel in the Ethereal Body. This is the wisdom of John the Baptist.

---

9   "The Guardian of the Threshold is our Satan... our internal beast, the source of all of our animal passions and brutal appetites... " —Samael Aun Weor, *The Revolution of Beelzebub*

10 See glossary.

11 See glossary.

Arcanum 20: Eleventh hour of Apollonius. The awakening of the dead. The angels, the cherubim and seraphim fly with the sound of wings whirring; there is rejoicing in heaven; the earth and the sun that surge from Adam awaken. This process belongs to the great Initiations of Major Mysteries, where only the terror of the law reigns.

Arcanum 21: Twelfth hour of Apollonius. The towers of fire are disturbed. This is the victorious entry into the limitless bliss of nirvana, where the master is eventually clothed with the resplendent robe of Dharmakaya,[12] or rather renounces the bliss of nirvana for the love of humanity, and becomes a bodhisattva[13] of compassion; one becomes a savior of wretched, suffering humanity, one becomes another part of the protective wall raised with the blood of martyrs. Samyak-sambuddhas, masters of perfection, renounce nirvana for the love of humanity. The Pratyeka Buddhas[14] when dressed with the glory of the robe of [their elemental form of] Dharmakaya[15] can no longer reincarnate to help man or humanity, because nirvana is the forgetting of the world and men forever. The Bodhisattvas Kuan-Shi-Yin, Tashi Lama, Buddha Gautama, and Christ always radiate their light over suffering humanity.

Now we start the course of Kabbalah. Let us study the 22 Major Arcana of the Tarot. Therefore this course will have 22 lectures. We hope that you will study and practice with patience and tenacity so that you will attain great realizations. We will start by studying the First Arcanum of the Tarot. We will enter into the sanctum regnum of high magic.

Inverential peace,
Samael Aun Weor

---

12 Body of truth. See glossary.
13 Incarnations of wisdom (Christ). See glossary.
14 "Selfish awakened beings." See glossary.
15 Read "A Talk on the Mysteries of Life and Death" in *Beyond Death* by Samael Aun Weor.

The Magician

ARCANUM 1

Arcanum 1

This Arcanum is represented by The Magician. The Holy Eight, symbol of the infinite, appears above the head of the magician; the Holy Eight encloses, defines, and joins the magnetic currents of the mind that deals with dream consciousness with the mind that deals with vigil consciousness. This sign joins or separates all of the elements which are controlled by the atomic energy, if it is traced with the middle finger, index finger and the thumb over the surface of the cardiac plexus.

Practice: According with the former description, the following exercise is suggested: withdraw all type of thoughts from your mind. Now imagine the Holy Eight as it is represented in the following graphic:

THE HOLY EIGHT, THE SYMBOL OF INFINITY

Allow the figure to sink into your consciousness, and thereafter, while falling asleep, empty your mind, without thinking of anything. Thus after a while, you will awaken your consciousness in the astral plane.[16]

If we consider the formation of this symbol, we see that it illustrates the continuity of only one arm that encloses a double circuit in the beginning of the stroke, while enclosing only one circuit in the continuation of the stroke. Thereafter, the stroke divides the sign at the point where it centrally crosses it and it then continues into the other circuit in order to project itself towards the exterior. One circuit closes and the other opens.

This is the required key in order to open all the doors and to cut all the currents formed by the atomic energy, beginning with the one that we have imagined and placed within the depth of our consciousness and ending with the one that

---

16 See glossary.

originated the rest, which circulates in the same manner in the center of the "Ninth Sphere."[17]

Now then, to overcome by means of these requirements the risks per se of every astral experience and thus to obtain a fast and also perfect astral projection is more than enough reason, among other things, in order for the Sacred Order of Tibet to affirm in its motto: "Nothing can resist our power."

Thus, moments before lying down in order to perform this practice, the disciple must invoke with all of his heart and with all of his soul the great regent of the Sacred Order of Tibet. The name of this great Guruji is Bhagavan Aklaiva. This order, which we have the honor of representing here in Mexico, is the most powerful order of all the Asian traditions. This order is formed by 201 members. The major rank is formed by seventy-two Brahmans.

Papus in his *Treatise of Occult Science* stated that the true initiates from the east are the ones who belong to the secret sanctuaries of Brahmanism, since they are the only ones who can give us the royal clue of the Arcanum A.Z.F.,[18] thanks to their knowledge of the primeval Atlantean language "Watan," the fundamental roots of Sanskrit, Hebrew, and Chinese.

The Sacred Order of Tibet is the genuine owner of the real treasury of Aryavarta. This treasury is the Arcanum A.Z.F.

Bhagavan Aklaiva will help you to consciously travel in your astral body. Invoke him when you are meditating on the sacred sign of the infinite. On any given night, you will be invoked from the temple of the Himalayas; there you will be submitted to "seven ordeals." There you will be taught the secret science.

Now then, after this digression, let us continue with our initial point. The Holy Eight symbolizes the Caduceus of Mercury and represents the two ganglionic chords that esoterically are entwined around the spinal medulla, these are: Ida and Pingala; the two witnesses, the olive branches, the two candlesticks standing before the god of the earth.

---

17 See page 66.
18 See glossary.

The solar atoms[19] rise through the cord of the right and the lunar atoms rise through the cord of the left.

These solar and lunar atoms rise from our seminal system; the fire of Phlegethon and the water of Acheron[20] cross in the Ninth Sphere, sex, and form the sign of the infinite.

F + A = C: fire plus water equals consciousness.

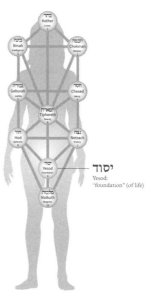

Whosoever meditates on the sign of the infinite will utilize the fire and the water in order to awaken the consciousness. Now we understand why the two witnesses of revelation have the power of prophecy.

> *"And I will give power unto my two witnesses, and they shall prophesy a thousand two hundred and threescore days, clothed in sackcloth. As we said: These are the two olive trees, and the two candlesticks standing before the God of the earth."*
> —Revelation 11:3, 4

Now then, the quantity 1,260 (a thousand two hundred and threescore days) is kabbalistically added as follows:

1 + 2 + 6 + 0 = 9; this is the symbol of the Ninth Sphere.

The Ninth Sphere is sex. The two witnesses have their root in the sex. These two witnesses Ida and Pingala are two fine ganglionic chords through which the solar and lunar atoms of our seminal system ascend to the "chalice." The chalice is the brain.

Fill your chalice, my brothers and sisters, with the sacred wine of light.

Now you comprehend why the sign of the infinite appears above the head of the magi-

---

19 See entries for atoms, lunar, and solar in the glossary.

20 In Greek mythology, these are rivers in Hades.

cian, and why the sword, the cup and pantacles are before him, and why is he grasping the magic wand that symbolizes the spinal medulla.

When the solar and lunar atoms make contact in the coccygeal bone, the Kundalini, the igneous serpent of our magical powers awakens, then we are devoured by the serpent and we convert ourselves into excellent divine magicians.

Arcanum 2

Now let us study the magical equilibrium of the Second Arcanum of the Tarot.

The physical body is organized by the elements. The Innermost emanated from the Inner Star that has always smiled upon us; He is positively polarized. The physical body is the negative shadow of the Innermost.

Spirit and matter live in eternal combat. When the Spirit defeats matter, the Spirit then becomes a master. Maya[21] (illusion) could not exist without duality. Force and matter are two modalities of the same thing: energy. Matter is determined energy and a determinator of new undulations. Evolution is a process of complication of energy, whose outcome is the Macrocosmos[22] and Microcosmos.[23] The universe is maya (illusion). The universe exists because of karma,[24] and it is a mass of floating shadows.

When the Spirit (the Innermost) liberates himself from maya, it returns to the Ain Soph[25] of Kabbalah. In the last synthesis, each being is just a super divine atom from the abstract absolute space. That atom is the Ain Soph.

The ineffable gods from the Ain Soph are beyond any comprehension for us. To the gods of the Ain Soph, the human mind is what the activities of the mineral kingdom are to us. Within the Ain Soph, only the unity of life reigns; that is supreme happiness.

---

21 (Sanskrit) Also a name for the Divine Mother.
22 (Greek) Macro means "great, large." Cosmos means "order, harmony, the world (from its perfect order and arrangement)." In Universal Gnosticism, the term Macrocosmos can refer to the universe in general, or specifically to a galaxy, which is one of seven levels of the whole creation.
23 (Greek) Micro means "small, little, trivial, slight." Cosmos means "order, harmony, the world (from its perfect order and arrangement)." In Universal Gnosticism, the term Microcosmos refers to the human being, who is a universe in minature.
24 (Sanskrit) Cause and effect.
25 Abstract space; that which is without attributes or limitations. Also known as sunyata, void, emptiness, Parabrahman, Adi-buddha, and many other names.

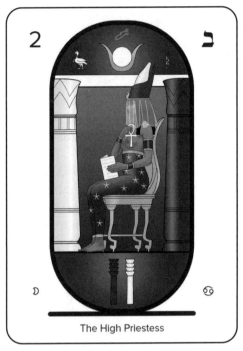

The High Priestess

ARCANUM 2

The universe is duality, maya/pain. We need to liberate ourselves from the binary and to return into the unity of life. It is urgent to pass beyond the painful manifestations of maya. There is a science with which we can tear the veil of maya and return into the Ain Soph; that science is Alchemy.

Dr. Arnold Krumm-Heller stated:

> "A chemist just happened to forget about an emerald ring that was close to a little test tube containing radium. After few weeks he saw that the emerald had absolutely changed into another stone, unknown to him. Thereafter he purposely left other stones like rubies, zephyrs, etc., in contact with the radium: his surprise was great when he discovered that after a little time such stones had absolutely changed their color; the

blue ones had turned into red and the red ones into green." '

Dr. Krumm-Heller continues saying,

"Gentlemen, do you know what the former statement that I just mentioned means (since I do not consider that it is scientifically established)? It means that Shakespeare was right when he said that 'many things exist between heaven and earth that our scholastic consciousness does not even suspect,' and the science of alchemy is reborn when corroborating the transmutations of metals."

Man and woman must equilibrate their forces; they must become alchemists so they can return to the Ain Soph. Circe offers the tempting cup and Ulysses rejects her with his sword.[26] The sacred sign of the infinite represents the brain, heart, and sex of the planetary genie. This struggle is terrible: brain against sex, and sex against brain, and what is even more terrible and more painful, heart against heart. You know this.

The masters used to place three cups of glory, three cups of Alchemy, upon the altars of the temples of the White Lodge.[27] Each one of these three sacred cups of the temple contains a precious balm: the Red Balm is the fire, the Blue Balm is the water, and the White Balm is the Universal Spirit of Life.

Ida and Pingala are the canals through which the atoms of fire and water ascend; the Spirit grasps the cane with seven knots (that cane is the spinal medulla). When man and woman learn how to avoid the sexual spasm and the ejaculation of the ens seminis,[28] then the igneous serpent of our magical powers awakens. If you want to return to the Father who is in secret, you must first return to the bosom of your Divine Mother Kundalini. You need to raise the serpent of life through your medullar canal. This is Alchemy.

---

26 A symbolic story from Homer's *Odyssey*.
27 See glossary.
28 (Latin) Literally, "the entity of semen." A term used by Paracelsus.

Alchemy: You have forgotten your Divine Mother Kundalini. You need to worship the divine and blessed Mother Goddess of the world. You have been ungrateful to your Cosmic Mother. She is the Virgin of all religious cults. She is Isis, Mary, Cybele, Adonia, Insobertha, etc. The stone of grace is surrounded by nine delectable mountains; that stone is sex. If you want to return to the bosom of your Divine Mother, you need to work with the Philosophical Stone: sex.

The Mayans stated that in the first heaven God, the Word, had held his stone, had held his serpent, and had held his substance. Only with the Arcanum A.Z.F. can the Word become flesh in order to grasp his stone, his serpent and his substance anew. Then we will return into the Ain Soph; we will return into the unity of life. You are the children of the Widow, your Divine Mother is now a widow, but when she rises through the medullar canal, she is betrothed with the Eternal Beloved. Your Divine Mother is the Second Arcanum, the Popess of the Tarot. She is crowned with a tiara. The head of the Divine Mother is surrounded by a veil. You must be courageous and lift the Veil of Isis. Our Gnostic motto is Thelema (willpower).

The Mother carries her son (the Word) within her arms; and she is seated between the two columns that symbolize man and woman. Worship the Virgin of the Sea, brothers and sisters of mine. The Divine Mother appears in the Second Arcanum making the priestly esoteric sign with her hand. Study within the sacred book of your Divine Mother.

> "Ask and it shall be given to you. Knock and it shall be opened unto you." –Matthew 7:7

Your Divine Mother can grant the longed for esoteric powers. Pray to your Divine Mother; practice your esoteric exercises; you can ask your adored Mother for clairvoyance, telepathy, clairaudience, the faculties for astral projection, etc. You can be sure that your Divine Mother will listen to your beseeching. You must profoundly meditate everyday upon your Divine Mother, praying, pleading. "You need to be devoured by the serpent." One (1) is the man, two (2) is the woman; the man is one column, the woman is the other column of the temple. The two columns must not be too close or too distant;

there must be enough space so that the light can pass between them.

It is necessary to transmute the lead of the personality into the pure gold of the spirit: this is Alchemy. The moon must be transformed into the sun. The moon is the Soul; the sun is the inner Christ. We need to be Christified. No human being can return to the Father without having been devoured by the serpent. No one can be devoured by the serpent without having worked in the flaming forge of Vulcan (sex). The key of Christification is the Arcanum A.Z.F. The mantra for the Arcanum A.Z.F. is I.A.O. – I (Ignis), Fire; A (Aqua), Water; O (Origo), Principle, Spirit.

Mars descends into the flaming forge of Vulcan in order to retemper his sword and to conquer the heart of Venus, Hercules descends in order to clean the stables of Augias with the sacred fire, and Perseus descends in order to cut off Medusa's head. Remember beloved disciples, that our Divine Mother is Nut, and her word is (56) fifty-six. This number is kabbalistically added as follows: 5 + 6 = 11, then 1 + 1 = 2. One is the Father; two is She, Nut, the Divine Mother Kundalini.

Practice

1. Lay down on your bed, facing up and with your relaxed body.
2. Achieve the state of slumber by meditating upon the sacred serpent that dwells in the coccygeal chakra.
3. Thereafter, pray with all of your heart, meditating on the following sacred, ritualistic prayer:

INVOCATION

Be thou, oh Hadit, my secret, the Gnostic mystery of my Being, the central point of my connection, my heart itself, and bloom on my fertile lips, made Word!

Up above, in the infinite Heavens, in the profound height of the unknowable, the incessant glow of light is the naked beauty of Nut. She reclines, she bends in delectable ecstasy, to receive the kiss of secret fervor of Hadit. The winged sphere and the blue of the sky are mine.

O.A.O. KAKOF NA. KHONSA

O.A.O. KAKOF NA. KHONSA

O.A.O. KAKOF NA. KHONSA

These mantras have the power of transmuting our sexual energy into light and fire within the alchemical laboratory of the human body. This prayer with its mantras can be utilized in Sexual Magic. This prayer with its mantras is an omnipotent clue in order to meditate upon our Divine Mother.

The Master Huiracocha (Dr. Krumm-Heller) stated the following in his *Rosicrucian Novel:*

> "When the man joins the woman in the secret
> act, he becomes a God since he converts himself
> into a Creator in this moment. Seers state that
> in those precise moments of love, the two beings
> are seen enveloped by a brilliant burst of light;
> they are enveloped by the most subtle and potent
> forces that are in nature. If man and woman
> would know how to withdraw without the spasm
> and retain such a vibration, then they can operate
> with it as a magician in order to purify themselves
> and obtain everything. However if they do not
> know how to retain such light, it will withdraw
> from them in order to set out into the universal
> currents, yet leaving behind the open doors so
> that evil can introduce itself to them. Then love is
> converted into hatred, their illusion is followed by
> deception."

With the mantric prayer that we have taught in this lesson, we retain that brilliant cosmic light that envelops the human couple in that supreme moment of love with the condition of avoiding, by all means, the ejaculation of the ens seminis. The mantras of this invocation have the power of transmuting the creative energies into light and fire.

The bachelor and bachelorettes can also transmute and sub-limate their sexual energies and carry them to the heart with this prayer and these mantras. You must know that in the tem-ple of the heart, the creative energies are mixed with the forces of Christ and thereafter they elevate to the superior worlds. The inner Christ lives in the heart temple. The cross of initia-tion is received in the heart temple. This mantric prayer is also a formula of priestly power that the magician utilizes in his practices of internal meditation in order to arrive at the feet of his Divine Mother. If the meditation is perfect, your beloved Mother will hear your call and she will come to you; then you can converse with her about ineffable, paradisiacal things. She is Devi Kundalini; She is the Popess of the Tarot. The Divine Mother always listens to her devotees. In the sacred land of the *Vedas*, Ramakrishna was one of her greatest devotees.

Do you want to reach the heights of Nirvikalpa-Samadhi? Do you need to develop Anubhava (perception of your Inner God in meditation)? Do you want the Jinn science?[29] Remember that you have an beloved Mother.

> *"Ask and it shall be given to you. Knock and it shall be opened unto you."* —Matthew 7: 7

---

29 The ability to move physical forms to and from the fourth dimension.

THE FIRST OF THE TWELVE KEYS OF BASIL VALENTINE.

Arcanum 3

Remember that the *Sepher Yetzirah*[30] marvelously describes all the splendors of the world and the extraordinary play of the sephiroth within God and the human being through the thirty-two paths of wisdom. The entire science of the sephiroth is hidden within the sexual mysteries.

The soul has three aspects:[31]

1. נפש Nephesh, the animal soul.
2. רוח Ruach, the thinking soul.
3. נשמת Neshamah, the spiritual soul.

The sephiroth are the substratum of these three aspects of the souls. The sephiroth are atomic.

The Zohar[32] insists on these three "principle elements" which compose the world. These elements are: fire (ש shin), water (מ mem), air (א aleph). These elements are the perfect synthesis of the four manifested elements.

The powerful mantra I.A.O. encompasses the magical power of the triangle of these principle elements:

I - Ignis - fire ש

A - Aqua - water מ

O - Origo - principle Spirit א

I.... A... O... is the supreme mantra of the Arcanum A.Z.F.

Whosoever wants to raise the soul of the world through the medullar canal must work with the Sulfur (Fire), with the Mercury (Water), and with the Salt (Philosophical Earth). It is only in this way that one can be born in Spirit and truth.

The twelve secret keys of Basil Valentine[33] (Basilius Valentinus), the Benedictine of Erfurt, are found within the Arcanum A.Z.F.

The entire secret of the Great Work is enclosed within the "Azoth" series of Basil Valentine. Azoth[34] is the sexual creative

---

30 A book of Kabbalah. Read at glorian.org
31 See glossary.
32 A book of Kabbalah. See glorian.org for excerpts and commentaries.
33 A legendary alchemist.
34 See glossary.

FROM THE AZOTH SERIES OF BASIL VALENTINE.

principle of Nature. The Magnum Work has been performed when the rose of the spirit blooms upon the cross of our body.

The three principle-elements are the three mother letters of the Hebrew alphabet. When one is practicing the Arcanum A.Z.F. one is working with these three principle-elements within the great laboratory of Nature. One works with Mercury, Sulfur, and Salt when one practices the Arcanum A.Z.F.; this is how the lead of the personality is transmuted into the gold of the Spirit; this is how we create the Golden Child of Alchemy within us.

These three principle-elements become manifested within the four elements of Nature. There is the heat of fire and air, the humidity of air and water, and the dryness of fire and earth.

These are the three principle-elements, the I.A.O., the Sulfur, Mercury, and Salt contained within the four elements of Nature. The elemental paradises of Nature are found within these principle-elements. The kabbalist-alchemist must learn how to use Sulfur, Mercury, and Salt.

The larvae of the astral body (incubi, succubi, basilisks, dragons, phantoms, etc.) are destroyed by putting sulfur powder inside of our shoes. Sulfur originates invisible vapors that rise in order to disintegrate these types of larvae. Malignant forms of thoughts and larvae enclosed within any room are disintegrated when one burns sulfur upon a flaming piece of charcoal.

Mercury serves in order to prepare Lustral Water.[35] The great astrologer Nostradamus spent many nights before a copper container filled with water. This is how, by looking within these waters, this great seer saw the future events that he left written in his famous prophesies.

If we add mercury to water and place a mirror at the bottom of the copper container, a marvelous "clairteleidoscope" is formed. We advise the use of any copper container with the exception of the so-called cauldron (a symbol of black magic). Copper is intimately related with the pituitary gland and has the power of awakening clairvoyance.

Salt is also used often in white magic. Salt must be combined with alcohol. If alcohol and salt are placed within a container and if this mixture is then ignited, a marvelous smoke offering is obtained. This type of smoke offering is only done when invoking the gods of medicine, when a sick person needs to be healed. Thus, they will attend to your call.

The sulfur (fire) totally burns without leaving any residue. Sulfur is the ש shin of the *Zohar*. The water (the ens seminis) is the מ mem of the *Zohar*. By means of successive transmutations,[36] fire and water are reduced to the kabbalistic א aleph (which the alchemist calls Alkaest). This is how the I.A.O. is performed, and this is how the twelve faculties of the soul are opened. The soul is Christified, "the Kundalini blooms upon our fertile lips made Word." The ternary is the Word, plenitude, fecundity, nature, the generation of the three worlds.

The Third Arcanum of Kabbalah is that woman dressed with the sun, with the moon under her feet, and crowned with twelve stars. The symbol of the Queen of Heaven is the Empress of the Tarot. She is a mysterious, crowned woman, seated with the scepter of command in her hand. The globe of the world is on top of the Scepter. She is Urania-Venus of the Greeks, the Christified Soul.

---

35 Holy Water.
36 "To change thoroughly," ie. lead into gold.

The Empress

ARCANUM 3

The man is Arcanum One, and the woman is Arcanum Two of the Tarot. The Christified soul is the outcome of their sexual union (the secret is the Arcanum A.Z.F.). The woman is the Mother of the Word. Christ is always the child of immaculate conceptions. It is impossible to be born without a mother.

When the initiate is ready to incarnate the Word, a woman appears in the superior worlds as if with child, having labor pains in delivery.

> "When Jesus therefore (on the cross) saw his mother and the disciple standing by, whom he loved, he said unto his mother: Woman, behold thy son! Then he said to (John) the disciple, Behold thy mother! And from that hour that disciple took her unto his own home." —John 19:26, 27

The word John can be rearranged as follows: I.E.O.U.A.N., the Word (the dragon of wisdom). Indeed, the woman is the mother of the Word and the woman officiates upon the altar of the blessed Goddess Mother of the world. Now brothers and sisters, know that the venerable priestess of your Divine Mother Kundalini is your spouse.

Brothers and sisters, pray and meditate a great deal to your Divine Mother Kundalini as follows:

INVOCATION

Oh Isis! Mother of the cosmos, root of love, trunk, bud, leaf, flower and seed of all that exists; we conjure thee, naturalizing force. We call upon the queen of space and of the night, and kissing her loving eyes, drinking the dew from her lips, breathing the sweet aroma of her body, we exclaim: Oh thou, Nut! Eternal Seity of heaven, who art the primordial soul, who art what was and what shall be, whose veil no mortal has lifted, when thou art beneath the irradiating stars of the nocturnal and profound sky of the desert, with purity of heart and in the flame of the serpent, we call upon thee!

Pray and meditate intensely. The Divine Mother teaches her children. This prayer must be performed while combining meditation with the state of slumber. Then as in a dream-vision, illumination emerges; thus the Divine Mother

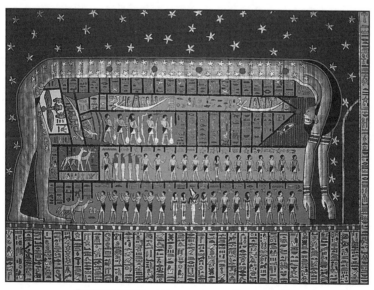

THE DIVINE MOTHER AS REPRESENTED BY THE EGYPTIANS AS NUT

approaches the devotee in order to give instruction in the great mysteries.

Arcanum 4

AUM. The Arcanum Four of the Tarot is the holy and mysterious Tetragrammaton,[37] the sacred name of the Eternal One that has four letters: Iod, Hei, Vav, Hei.

TETRAGRAMMATON

י Iod is the man, ה Hei is the woman, ו Vav is the phallus, ה Hei is the uterus. Yet, we can also state: י Iod is the man, ה Hei is the woman, ו Vav is the fire, ה Hei is the water. The profound study of the four letters of the Eternal One takes us inevitably to the Ninth Sphere (sex). We must lift our serpent through the medullar canal and carry it up to her heart's sanctuary.

The cross of the initiation is received in the heart temple. The magnetic center of the Father is found between the eyebrows. The sanctuary of the Mother is found within the heart temple. The four points of the cross symbolize the fire, the air, the water, and the earth (also Spirit, matter, movement, and repose).

Remember, beloved disciple, that the four elements of Alchemy are Salt, Mercury, Sulfur, and Azoth: Salt is matter, Mercury is the ens seminis, Azoth is the mysterious ray of Kundalini.

The Mercury of secret philosophy must be fecundated by Sulfur (fire) so that the Salt can become regenerated. Only like this can we write the book of Azoth; write it upon a reed if what you want is initiation. The clue of our liberation is found in the lingam-yoni.[38]

The cross has four points. The cross of initiation is phallic. The insertion of the vertical phallus into the formal cteis[39]

---

37 A Greek word referring to the Hebrew name of God, the Holy Four-lettered Name.

38 Lingam is a Sanskrit epithet for the male sexual organ, while yoni is for the female sexual organ.

39 (Greek κτείς Kteis) Alternatively spelled "ecteis." Literally, "comb" (of a loom), used for "rake, horn, fingers, ribs, scallop, vagina, yoni."

forms a cross. This is the cross of initiation that we must place upon our shoulders.

The four sacred animals of Alchemy are the lion that hides the enigma of fire; the man that represents the Mercury of secret philosophy; the eagle that corresponds to the air; the bull that symbolizes the earth. Egypt's sphinx (as well as Ezekiel's sphinx) has the sacred symbolism of the four creatures of alchemy.

When heated by the fire of the sun, the water contained in the lakes, rivers, and oceans is transformed into clouds that ascend up to the sky, and after a period of digestion are converted into lightning and thunder. This same process is repeated in the sexual laboratory of the alchemist. Our motto is Thelema[40] (willpower).

The entrance into the old, archaic temples was commonly a hidden hole in some mysterious spot in the dense jungle. We departed from Eden[41] through the door of sex, and only through that door can we return to Eden. Eden is sex. It is the narrow, straight, and difficult door that leads us into the light.

In the solitude of these mysterious sanctuaries, the neophytes were submitted to the four initiatic ordeals. The ordeals of fire, air, water, and earth always defined the diverse purifications of the neophytes.

Commonly, these sanctuaries of mysteries were found located at the foot of some volcano. There the disciples would fall to the ground and lose consciousness; in those moments the hierophant would take the students out of their physical bod-

---

40 Greek θέλημα) Willpower. "Father, if thou be willing, remove this cup from me: nevertheless not my will (Thelema), but thine, be done." —Luke 22: 42

41 The garden of Eden described by Moses in Bereshit / Genesis. The Hebrew word עדן literally means "bliss, pleasure, delight."

ies (thus, they would already be in the astral plane) and into the profundities of the sanctuary. Then he would teach them the grandiose mysteries of life and death. The volcanic emanations of the earth produced that apparent state of death. Some disciples fall in that apparent state of death within the Gnostic lumisials. The ceremony of carrying the cross (as was practiced in the Gnostic lumisials) serves in order to humbly confirm some internal, esoteric initiation.

Each one of the seven bodies[42] of the human being must be crucified and stigmatized.

---

42 The lower seven sephiroth correspond to the lower seven bodies of the Being.

THE TREE OF LIFE AND THE SEVEN BODIES

Absolute / Sunyata / Emptiness

Ain
Ain Soph
Ain Soph Aur

7th or Zero dimension — Kether — Dharmakaya, The Reality Body

Nirmanakaya, Emanation Body — Binah — Chokmah — Sambhogakaya, Perfect Resource Body

Daath

6th dimension — The Buddhic Body, The Divine Soul — 6 Geburah — 7 Chesed — The Atmic Body, The Innermost

5 Tiphereth — The Causal Body, The Human Soul

5th dimension — The Astral Body — 3 Hod — 4 Netzach — The Mental Body

4th dimension

2 Yesod — The Vital Body

3rd dimension — 1 Malkuth — The Physical Body

Lower 5th dimension — Subconsciousness, Unconsciousness, Infraconsciousness

THE FOUR GOSPELS. CAROLINGIAN DEPICTION FROM AN AACHEN GOSPEL, 820

All students of Kabbalah must be familiar with all of the elementals[43] of fire, air, water, and earth. The present "human being" is still not a king or queen of Nature, but all are called to be kings or queens and priests and priestesses according to the order of Melchizedeck.[44]

It is necessary for the student to become familiar with all the elemental creatures of the four elements. Salamanders live in fire. Undines and nereids live in water. Sylphs live in the air, and gnomes live in the earth.

The gospel of Mark is symbolized by a lion (fire); the gospel of Matthew is represented by a youth (water); the gospel of John is represented by the eagle (air) and the gospel of Luke is represented by the bull (earth). The four gospels symbolize the

---

43 See glossary.
44 See glossary.

four elements of nature and the realization of the Great Work (the Magnus Opus).

Every hierophant of Nature is converted into a king of the elementals. If you want to be admitted into the elemental paradises of Nature, then respect all life, do not kill any animal species, do not drink wine that contains alcohol; love vegetables, do not ever destroy a plant or a flower. You only need two things in life: wisdom and love. This is how you will attain happiness, peace, and abundance.

> "Be ye therefore perfect, even as your Father which is in heaven is perfect." —Matthew 5:48

Every initiate must work with the elementals in the central mountain range. That mountain range is the spinal medulla. The prima matter of the Great Work of the Father is the ens seminis. You know this.

The sacred receptacle is in your creative organs, the furnace is the Muladhara chakra,[45] the chimney is the medullar canal, and the distiller is the brain. When we work in the laboratory of the Third Logos we must transmute the lead of our personality into the gold of the Spirit. The Magnus Work cannot be performed without the cooperation of the elementals.

The gnomes and pygmies are the great alchemists that transmute the lead into gold; they reduce the metals to its semen (seed) in order to transmute them into the pure gold of the spirit; their labor would be impossible if the undines did not obey or if the salamanders of fire would not make the voluptuous undines fertile, because without the fire, the tempting undines can only take us to a shipwreck. Ulysses (the cunning warrior destroyer of citadels) was himself bound to the mast of the ship so that he would not fall seduced by the sexual beauty of the undines. Ancient Gnostics stated: "All of you will become gods if you leave Egypt and pass through the Red Sea (the ocean of temptations)."

The vapors of the prima matter of the Great Work would not ascend through the chimney without the help of the

---

45 Muladhara (Sanskrit) lit. "root and basis of existence." The root chakra located near the base of the spine. Church: Ephesus. Vowel: S.

disquieting sylphs. The gnomes need to distil the gold in the brain and this is only possible with the help of the aerial sylphs. The gnomes transmute the lead into gold. The Magnus Opus would be impossible without the elementals. We need to become familiar with the elementals of Nature.

Practice

FIRE: light a fire, then vocalize the mantra **INRI**.[46] This mantra is vocalized in two separate syllables: IN – RI:

Prolong the sound of each letter.

IiiiiiiiiiiiiNnnnnnnnn RrrrrrrrrrrIiiiiiiiiiiiiii

Thereafter, concentrate on the fire that you have lit (on the candle, on the oil lamp, or on the charcoal) and profoundly meditate on the fire. Invoke me, Samael, your friend, who wrote this lecture. I will assist you in this practice. Then vocalize the "S" as an affable and fine whistle, like the buzzing of a rattlesnake.

Practice with the Sylphs

AIR: seated on a comfortable chair or laying down (face up) with the body relaxed, you will profoundly meditate on the following plagiary:

> *Spiritus Dei Ferebatur super aquas, et inspiravit in faciem hominis spiraculum vitae.*
> *Sit Michael Dux Meus, et Sabtabiel servus meus, in luce et per lucem. Fiat verbum halitus meus, et imperabo Spiritibus aeris hujus, et refrenabo equos solis voluntate cordis mei, et cogitatione mentis mei et nutu oculi dextri. Exorciso igitur te, creatura aeris, per Pentagrammaton et in nomine Tetragrammaton, in quibus sunt voluntas firma et fides recta. Amen. Sela Fíat.*

Blow towards the four cardinal points of the Earth. Pronounce the letter H many times as if imitating a very deep

---

46   The vowel I is pronounced as in Latin, such as the i in "machine."

sigh. Then slumber while meditating on the genii Michael and Sabtabiel. This way you will become in contact with the sylphs.

Practice with the Undines

WATER: before a cup of water, get into the state of slumber while meditating on the following exorcism:

EXORCISM

Fiat firmamentum in medio aquarum et separet aquas ab aquis, quae superius sicut quae inferius, et quae inferius sicut quae superius ad perpetranda miracula rei unius. Sol ejus pater est, luna mater et ventus hanc gestavit in utero suo, ascendit a terra ad coelum et rursus a chelo in terram descendit exorciso te creatura aquae, ut sis mihi peculum die vivi in operibus ejus, et fons vitae, et abllutio pecatorum. Amen.

Thereafter, while still in a state of slumber, vocalize the letter **M** as follows: *Mmmmmmmm*, with your lips hermetically sealed. This sound is like the bellow of the bull, yet it is a prolonged sustained sound that does not decrease like the bull does. The letter "M" is the mantra of the waters. This is how you will be in contact with the creatures of the waters. Thereafter, invoke the genie of the waters; the genie's name is Nicksa.

Practice with the Gnomes

EARTH: Profoundly meditate on the heart temple of the center of the Earth. Meditate on the genie of the Earth whose name is Cham-Gam. Beseech him to place you in contact with the gnomes that inhabit the entrails of the Earth; call the genie of the gnomes, the genie's name is GOB. Get into a state of slumber while concentrating on that genie; then vocalize the mantra **I.A.O.**

ARCANUM 4 FROM THE ETERNAL TAROT

Iiiiiiiiiiiiiiiiiiiiiiiiiiiiiiiiiiiiiii AaaaaaaaaaaaaaaaaaaaaaaaaaaaaOooo oooooooooooooooo

When profound meditation is intelligently combined with the state of slumber, it allows you to enter into the elemental paradises of Nature.

Every alchemist needs to work with the elementals of Nature.

The hieroglyphic of the Fourth Arcanum of the Tarot is the Emperor; the sovereign appears forming a marvelous triangle with his body. When the legs of the Emperor are crossed, they form a cross; this is the image of the athanor of alchemists; the joint of the cross with a triangle is only possible by means of the potable gold (sacred fire) of alchemy.

ALCHEMICAL SYMBOL OF SULFUR (FIRE)

The Innermost puts the cross of initiation with the Arcanum Four of the Tarot over his shoulder.

We will end this lecture by stating that the elementals of fire are commanded with the trident of iron or with the wand of iron; the elemental of the air are commanded with an eagle feather or any other bird; the elementals of water are commanded with a cup filled with water and the elementals of the Earth with a sword or with a new knife.

The main kingdom of the gnomes resides in the North; the one of the salamanders in the South, the one of the sylphs in the East and the one of the undines in the West. These four elemental hierarchies form a cross. Behold here, the holy and mysterious Tetragrammaton.

ARCANUM 4 FROM THE TAROT
DE MARSEILLE (CA. 1890)

The Hierarch

Arcanum 5

Beloved brothers and sisters of my soul, today we are going to study the Fifth Arcanum of the Tarot. This arcanum is the flaming pentagram, the blazing star, the sign of divine omnipotence. This is the ineffable symbol of the Word made flesh, the terrifying star of the Magi.

When the pentagram elevates its two inferior rays towards the sky it represents Satan.[47]

When the pentagram becomes light, it elevates only one of its rays towards the sky; this represents the internal Christ of every human being who comes into this world.

The human being with his legs and arms spread out to the right and left is the star of five points. Brain and sex live in an eternal struggle. Brain must control sex. When sex overcomes the brain, then the star of five points (the human being) falls into the abyss with the feet pointing upwards and the head pointing downwards; this is the inverted star, the male goat of Mendes. A human figure with the head aiming downwards and the feet aiming upwards naturally represents a demon.

PENTAGRAM

The entire science of Gnosis is found summarized within the flaming star. Many bodhisattvas[48] have fallen inverted, like the five pointed star, with the superior ray aiming downwards and the two inferior rays aiming upwards.

When any of these bodhisattvas rise again, when this soul returns to the path, when this soul recapitulates initiations, then the brothers and sisters become astonished and say, "This fellow is only a beginner in these studies and now he boasts of being an initiate." Truly, many times students judge *a priori* because they ignore the great mysteries. Therefore, we must

---

47 Adversary. See glossary.
48 Human souls of masters. See glossary.

know how to differentiate between a soul that is just starting these studies and a fallen bodhisattva.

In Saint John's Revelation 8:10, the pentagram (the five pointed star) falls from heaven (burning as if it were a lamp) and the human waters became bitter, they became wormwood. In Isaiah 14:12, the prophet said:

> "How art thou fallen from heaven, O shiny star
> (Lucifer), son of the morning? How art thou cut down
> to the ground?"

Nevertheless, the luciferic star (the fallen soul) will shine one day as the morning star in the right hand of the Word.

Many times a man or a woman in search of the divine torch of truth arrives at some Gnostic lumisial; apparently the newly arrived is now a beginner, however, the brothers and sisters ignore what the soul of that person is; he or she can be a bodhisattva (the human soul of a master) that wants to return to his own Father who is in secret. Thus, the brothers and sisters become overwhelmed when something superior occurs to the apparent beginner, then they say: "We, who are longer in these studies, are not passing through what this beginner is now passing through," thus, they ask themselves: "How is it possible that this person who has only just begun is boasting about being an initiate?"

> "Judge not, that ye be not judged. For with what
> judgment ye judge, ye shall be judged: and with what
> measure ye mete, it shall be measured to you again."
> —Matthew 7:1-2

We need to be humble in order to acquire wisdom, and after acquiring it we need to be even more humble. The bodhisattvas fall because of sex, and they also rise up because of sex. Sex is the Philosophical Stone. The decapitation of Medusa[49] (the Satan that we carry within) would be impossible without the precious treasury of the Philosophical Stone. Remember that Medusa is the maiden of evil (the psychological "I"), whose head is covered with hissing vipers. In esoteric science, it is stated that the union of the Sophic mercury with the Sophic

---

49 Greek symbol of our psychological defects.

Sulfur results in the holy Philosophical Stone. The ens seminis is the Mercury. Sulfur is the sacred fire of love.

We live now in the specific age of Samael; we live in the fifth era.[50]

Life has initiated its return towards the Great Light and in these moments we have to define ourselves by becoming eagles or reptiles, angels or demons. We are before the philosophical dilemma of "to be or not to be."

The Arcanum Five of the Tarot is represented by the Hierophant. The fifth sphere is definitive because here the human being holds in his hands the reins of his own destiny and becomes an angel or a demon.

Arcanum 5 from the Tarot de Marseille (ca. 1890)

The great hierophant of the Tarot also appears seated between the two columns of the temple making the sign (the pentagram) of esotericism.

The number five is grandiose, sublime. Remember that the human being is also a star of five points; this human star must cleanse itself constantly with the five perfumes.[51] If we can make a metallic pentagram and consecrate it, we can also consecrate ourselves with the same rites and perfumes that we use to consecrate our metallic pentagram. This is because the human being is a star of five points.

Those who feel that they are polluted with larvae, or in misery, must smudge themselves with the five perfumes in order to become clean. This must be performed in conjunction with treading on the path of perfect chastity. In the lumisials, this custom of cleansing the brothers and sisters that are full of larvae should be established. Thus, they will receive the benefit in their souls and in their bodies.

---

50 Each root race is guided by a Logos. Previous to use, there was the Polar (Gabriel), Hyperborean (Raphael), Lemurian (Uriel), and Atlantean (Michael).

51 Frankincense, myrrh, aloe, sulphur, and camphor.

Indecision

ARCANUM 6 OF THE ETERNAL TAROT

Arcanum 6

Beloved brothers and sisters of my soul: we are now going to study the Sixth Arcanum of the Tarot.

Beloved, remember that indeed without any doubt, the two interlaced triangles of the Seal of Solomon, which join or separate love, are the two shuttles with which the ineffable mystery of eternal life in the loom of God is woven or unwoven. The upper triangle symbolizes Kether (the Father who is in secret), Chokmah (the Son), and Binah (the Holy Spirit of each human being). The lower triangle represents the three traitors of Hiram Abiff; those three traitors are inside of us. The first traitor is the demon of desire; that traitor lives within the astral body. The second traitor is the demon of the mind; that traitor lives within the mental body. The third traitor is the demon of evil will; that traitor lives within the body of willpower (causal body). The Bible cites these three traitors in the Apocalypse of Saint John in Revelation 16:13, 14:

> *"And I saw three unclean spirits like frogs come out of the mouth of the dragon, and out of the mouth of the beast, and out of the mouth of the false prophet; for they are the spirits of devils, working miracles, which go forth unto the kings of the earth and of the whole world, to gather them to the battle of that great day of God Almighty (El-Shaddai)."*

The three traitors constitute the reincarnating ego, the psychological "I," the Satan that must be dissolved in order to incarnate the inner Christ, which is constituted by Kether, Chokmah, and Binah. The superior triangle is the resplendent dragon of wisdom, whereas the inferior triangle is the black dragon.

The sign of the infinite or the tau cross are found in the center of the two triangles; both are phallic (sexual) signs. The soul is found between the two triangles and has to decide between the white dragon and the black dragon. That dilemma is absolutely sexual.

The clue is found in the serpent. In the Abraxas,[52] the rooster's legs are made by the double tail of a serpent. The tempting serpent of Eden exists as well as Moses' serpent of brass (nachash) interlaced around the tau, in other words, entwined around the sexual lingam (the phallus); the yoni is the uterus.

ABRAXAS

Normally, the serpent is enclosed within the chakra Muladhara (church of Ephesus). The serpent slumbers in that coccygeal center entwined three and a half times. The serpent must inevitably leave from its church. If the serpent rises through the medullar canal we convert ourselves into angels and if the serpent descends we convert ourselves into demons. Now you can comprehend why there are always two serpents around the Caduceus of Mercury. The sexual force is the Hyle[53] of the Gnostics.

When the students spill the cup of Hermes during their practices with the Arcanum A.Z.F. they commit the crime of the Nicholaitans, which used a system in order to make the serpent descend. This is how the human being is converted into a demon.

The complete and positive development of the serpent is only achieved by working with the Philosophical Stone within the sexual laboratory of the practical alchemist.

The superior triangle is the center of the alchemist's microcosmos and the alchemist's macrocosmos. The sign of the Mercury of the secret philosophy (the ens seminis) cannot be missed in the center of the triangle. Man and woman must

---

52 "Mystical term used by the Gnostics to indicate the supreme entity of our cosmic hierarchy or its manifestation in the human being which they called the Christos."

53 Primordial matter. "The elements are made out of hyle and every element is converted into the nature of another element." —Roger Bacon

work with the Sun and with the Moon, with the Gold and with the Silver (sexual symbols) in order to perform the Great Work. Nevertheless, this work is very difficult because the male goat of Mendes (the black dragon) always tries to make the alchemist sexually fall. It is urgent to work with the four elements of alchemy in order to perform the Great Work.

The alchemical macrocosmos is illuminated by the Light; this is the superior triangle of the Seal of Solomon. The alchemical microcosmos is in the shadows, in the region where the souls fight against the black dragon.

It is precisely in the microcosmos, represented by the inferior triangle, where the entire work of alchemical laboratory must be performed by us.

FROM CHIMICA BASILICA PHILOSOPHICA

The marvelous microcosmic and macrocosmic alchemical illustration above (from *Chimica Basilica Philosophica*) represents the man and the woman working with the Sun (the symbol of the phallus) and with the Moon (the symbol of the uterus). In this medieval painting, two men together or two women together do not appear because such a crime against Nature only creates a filthy vampire. The tenebrous ones justify their crimes against Nature, thus the law punishes them by separating them from their superior triangle forever. This is how they roll into the abyss.

The mysteries of lingam-yoni are terribly divine and cannot be altered. The lingam can only be united with the yoni; this is the law of holy alchemy. The alchemical weddings signify, as a fact, a perfect matrimony.

The alchemist must not only kill desire, but moreover, he has to kill the very shadow of the horrible tree of desire.

Sacred dances between men and women were performed in the mysteries of Eleusis along with love and the music of the centers in order to enchant the serpent. Then, the dancers of the temple were clean from the filthy venom of desire. All kind of sins are forgiven, except the sins against the Holy Spirit.

> "Flee fornication. Every sin that a man does is without the body; but he that commits fornication sin against his own body." —1 Corinthians 6:18

However, fornication[54] does not pertain only to the physical body; it is also related to thoughts, emotions, words, and animal sensations.

In the mysteries of Eleusis, the couples danced in order to magnetize each other; then while dancing, the couple (man and woman) together attained ecstasy. The bio-electromagnetic interchange between man and woman cannot be replaced by anything; this is a gigantic, grandiose and terribly divine power. God shines upon the perfect couple.

If you want in-depth realization of your Self, remember this alchemical aphorism:

> "Nature contains nature: Nature overcomes nature: and Nature meeting with her nature, exceedingly rejoices, and is changed into other natures."
>
> — Roger Bacon, Mirror of Alchemy

The task of the alchemist is to search for the esoteric and ancient knowledge and to perform the Great Work in his sexual laboratory. The Great Work is difficult, it signifies many years of experiments, terrible sacrifices, and tremendous difficulties. There are a transmutator agent (the Philosophical

---

54 Abuse of sexual energy, such as by orgasm. See glossary.

Stone), a heavenly influence (cosmic religiosity), diverse astral influences (esoteric astrology), influence of letters, numbers, correspondences, sympathies (Kabbalah).

The sacred principles of Alchemy are:
- Unity
- A pair of opposites (man/woman; active/passive)
- Trinity (active, passive, neutral)
- The elements (fire, air, water, and earth)

The entire work of the Great Work (the Magnus Opus) is united in the Seal of Solomon. The six points of the star are masculine; the six outer obtuse angles that exist between point and point are feminine. In synthesis, this star has twelve rays: six masculine and six feminine. The Star of Solomon is

MASCULINE POINT

FEMININE INDENTATION

the perfect symbol of the central Sun, all of the zodiacal measurements are found summarized within the Seal of Solomon. The entire sexual Genesis of the zodiac is hidden in the Seal of Solomon. The inner relation between the zodiac and the invincible central Sun is found in the Seal of Solomon. The twelve rays of the brilliant star crystallize by means of Alchemy in the twelve zodiacal constellations.

When the student enters into the temple of the Sphinx one studies the great book of Nature, where all of the cosmic laws are written. Indeed, very few are the ones who can open the book and study it. The "ordeal of the sanctuary" is very terrible. Very few are the human beings who have succeeded in passing such an ordeal. A precious jewel (with the Seal of Solomon), a ring filled with ineffable light is granted to the one who victoriously passes the ordeal of the sanctuary. The neophyte who touches the ring with the left hand loses it inevitably.

Another explanation of the Seal of Solomon is the following; above: the Father, the Son, and the Holy Spirit; below: the power that governs (the Innermost), the power that deliberates (the mind), and the power that executes (the personality).

When the power that deliberates and the power that executes rebel or are subordinate against the governor (the Innermost) then the outcome is failure.

The three traitors use to take possession of the powers that deliberate and the powers that execute. The bodhisattvas sometimes used to receive[55] messages from the superior worlds; nevertheless, ignoramuses mistake the bodhisattvas with the mediums of Spiritism ("channelers").

There are mediums and mediators. The medium is negative, whereas the mediator is positive. The medium is a vehicle of the tempting serpent of Eden. The bodhisattva, the mediator, is a vehicle of the serpent of brass (nachash) that healed the Israelites in the wilderness.

Great masters used to dictate messages through the lips of their bodhisattvas. People do not understand this and mistake the mediators with the detrimental mediums of Spiritism, because people allow themselves to be carried away by false appearances.

The entire positive and negative forces of universal magnetism are found represented in the Seal of Solomon.

In the works of high magic, it is necessary to trace a circle around us. That circle must be totally closed, interrupted by the Seal of Solomon.

With the seven metals, Gnostic brothers and sisters can manufacture medallions and rings with the Seal of Solomon. The Seal of Solomon must be utilized in all of the works of invocations, and in the practices with elementals (as we have already taught in Arcanum Four of this series of lectures on Kabbalah).

The elementals of nature tremble before the seal of the living God.

The angel of the sixth seal of the Apocalypse has reincarnated at this time within a feminine body (this angel is a specialist in the sacred Jinn science).

---

55   In Hebrew, kabbel, "to receive," the root of the word Kabbalah.

Arcanum 6 is the Lover of the Tarot. It is the soul between vice and virtue. The Arcanum Six is enchainment, equilibrium, amorous union between man and woman, terrible struggles between love and desire, the mysteries of lingam-yoni, connection. The struggle between the two ternaries is found in the Sixth Arcanum of the Tarot. The Sixth Arcanum is the supreme affirmation of the internal Christ, and the supreme negation of Satan.

Watch and pray.

ALCHEMICAL LABORATORY FROM AMPHITHEATRUM SAPIENTIAE
AETERNAE (1602) BY HEINRICH KHUNRATH

The word laboratory comes from Latin: laboritorum, from labor, "to exert
with hardship, pain, fatigue," and oratorium "a place of prayer." There are
many lines converging on the very center of the image, passing through an
arch of four pillars. These four pillars are the four elements, the four bodies,
the cross, the four letters of the holy name of God. All the lines ultimately
point towards an open door. And what is behind the open door? A bed!
The bed is where the sexual act is performed. Our laboritorium, the place of
prayer where the work is performed, is the bedroom.

Arcanum 7

Remember that the number seven represents magical power in all of its strength.

The Holy Seven is the Sanctum Regnum[56] of Sexual Magic; the number seven is the Innermost served by all of the elemental forces of Nature.

Everyone who works with the Arcanum A.Z.F. receives the flaming sword of the Seventh Arcanum. In the name of truth, we affirm that the flaming sword of the great hierophants is absolutely transmuted semen, it is the outcome of Sexual Magic. This is how we transform ourselves into terribly divine gods.

The sexual organs are the legitimate laboratorium oratorium of the *Amphitheatrum Sapientiae Aeternae* [see illustration, opposite. These are the Sanctum Regnum where the hierophant receives the sword of justice.

In the alchemical *Garden of Pleasures,*[57] we find the word "Vitriol." This word is an acrostic, derived from the phrase "Visita interiora terra rectificando invenias occultum lapi-

---

56 Latin, "holy kingdom."
57 *Viridarium Chymicum* (1624) by Daniel Stolcius von Stolcenberg.

VITRIOL, FROM *VIRIDARIUM CHYMICUM* (1624)

dum," (Visit the interior of our earth, that by rectifying, you will find the esoteric stone).

We must search within the interior of our philosophical earth (the human organism); then by rectifying and working with the Arcanum A.Z.F., the Maithuna, we will find the Philosophical Stone.

The sun (phallus), masculine principle, is the father of the Stone. The moon (uterus) is the feminine principle, the mother of the Philosophical Stone. The wind bears the son in its womb and the earth nourishes it. The Sun and the Moon, masculine and feminine principles are combined inside of the chalice (symbol of the mind). The Sun (fire) is the Father of the Stone, the Moon (water) is the Mother, and the Wind (seminal steam) bear the son in its Alchemical Womb and the Philosophical Earth nourishes it.[58]

The chalice is resting on the Caduceus of Mercury (the central system, spinal column) with the two sympathetic cords known in the east as Ida and Pingala.

Two influences interact in the generation of the Philosophical Stone: one of a masculine character and the other of a feminine character.

The entire work is performed with the Great Arcanum. The star of seven points is an inseparable part of the acrostic VITRIOL. The seven serpents of Alchemy are related with the seven planets and the seven great cosmic realizations.

The acrostic VITRIOL with its seven letters and its seven words symbolizes the entire septenary Great Work that shines like the sun in the temple of science.

The sun and the moon, the fire and the water, the king and the queen form an integral part of any alchemist fledgling.

The fledgling has to perform seven great works that culminate with the crowing of the Great Work.

According to the illustration of *Viridarium Chymicum,* the face of a venerable elder appears in the center of the septenary star of Alchemy. That venerable face in the septenary star of Alchemy symbolizes the Sophic Mercury (the ens seminis).

---

58   This paragraph is paraphrased from *The Emerald Tablet* of Hermes Trismesgistus.

Listen, fledglings of Alchemy, listen to how Stolcius[59] explains this emblem:

> *"That which was enclosed within many forms, now*
> *you see it included in one thing; the beginning is our*
> *Elder and he has the key; sulfur with salt and mercury*
> *give wealth. If you do not see anything here, there is no*
> *reason for you to keep searching, for you will be blind*
> *even in the midst of the light."*

Those students of esotericism who think that they can acquire in depth realization of the Self without the Arcanum A.Z.F. are absolutely mistaken. The "secret sister master"[60] stated that those who want to know the mysteries of Chiram (the fire) must search among the Medieval alchemists. This great master was a true yogini disciple of Kout Humi;[61] nevertheless, after she had been widowed (by the Count Blavatsky) she married the Colonel Olcott in order to work with the arcanum of Sexual Magic. Only thus could she achieve in depth realization of the Self.

The great yogavatar[62] Sri Lahiri Mahasaya[63] was called to initiation by the immortal Babaji when he already had a spouse. Thus, this is how the yogavatar was Self-realized. In Hindustan, Sexual Magic is known by the Sanskrit term oordhvareta,[64] and the yogis who practice it are named oordha-vareta yogis.

Authentic yogis practice Sexual Magic with their spouse. There are two types of brahmacharya:[65] solar and lunar. The solar type is for those that have performed the Second

---

59 Daniel Stolcius von Stolcenberg (1600-1660)
60 Helena Petrovna Blavatsky (1831-1891)
61 "The great masters of the guardian wall that protect humanity live with the same physical bodies from millions of years ago, namely the Masters Kout Humi, Morya, and many others..." —Samael Aun Weor, *The Major Mysteries*
62 Sanskrit, "incarnation of yoga."
63 (1828-1895)
64 or Urdhvareta. Sanskrit; urdhva ,"upwards" + reta, "seed" thus literally meaning "to send the seed upwards."
65 Sexual abstention.

Triumph

ARCANUM 7 FROM THE ETERNAL TAROT

Birth.[66] The lunar type of brahmacharya is that absurd sexual abstinence that serves only to produce filthy, nocturnal sexual pollutions with all of its fatal consequences.

Hatha Yoga is just a matter of acrobatics that have the power of taking the student out of the superior worlds in order to enslave him to the physical world. We have never known of an acrobatic Hatha yogi with internal illuminated powers.

There are three rays of inner illumination of the realization of the Inner Self: the yogic, the mystic, and the perfect matrimony; however, the three rays inevitably need Sexual Magic. Anything that is not directed through Sexual Magic is a useless waste of time. We departed from Eden through the doors of

---

66   "... the fabrication of the solar bodies and the incarnation of the Being are known as the Second Birth." - Samael Aun Weor, *The Esoteric Treatise of Hermetic Astrology*

sex, and only through those doors can we return to Eden. Eden is sex itself.

The Seventh Arcanum is represented by a crowned warrior that carries a triangle above his crown, and he is standing upon the cubic stone of Yesod (sex). The two sphinxes, a white one and a black one, are pulling his chariot; this symbolizes the masculine and feminine forces. His armor is the divine science that makes us powerful. The warrior must learn how to use the staff and the sword, thus he will attain the great victory (Netzach). Our motto is Thelema (willpower).

Let us remember that there are seven vices that we must transmute into wisdom and love:

Lunar avarice is transformed into hope and altruism.

Laziness is transmuted into prudent Mercurian diligence.

The fatal Venusian lust is transmuted into the chastity of Venus and charity of the Spirit.

Pride must be transmuted into solar faith and into the humility of Christ.

Martian anger is transmuted into the marvelous force of love.

Envy is transmuted into Jupiterian philanthropy and happiness for others.

Gluttony is transmuted into Saturnian temperance.

We can disintegrate our defects and dissolve the psychological "I," only by means of the science of transmutations. Work with the Arcanum A.Z.F. so that you can receive the sword.

The governors of the seven planets are:

1. Gabriel: Moon
2. Raphael: Mercury
3. Uriel: Venus
4. Michael: Sun
5. Samael: Mars
6. Zachariel: Jupiter
7. Orifiel: Saturn

The seven notes of the lyre of Orpheus[67] correspond to the seven planets. A planetary note corresponds to each of the

---

67   Greek mythological symbol who used music to perform heroic feats.

seven colors of the solar prism. Alchemy is intimately related to music.

DETAIL FROM THE FRONTSPIECE OF *ATALANTA FUGIENS* (1618) BY MICHAEL MAIER, AN
ALCHEMICAL TEXT AND MUSICAL SCORE, "THE WHOLE TO BE SEEN, READ, MEDITATED,
UNDERSTOOD, JUDGED, SUNG, AND HEARD WITH EXTRAORDINARY PLEASURE."

Atalanta is the voice that flies ahead, Hippomenes is the voice that pursues, and the apple is the voice that delays.[68]

IAO

I.A.O. is the supreme mantra of Sexual Magic. I.A.O. is the name of the serpent. Blessed be the I.A.O.

I.A.O. must be chanted during the practices of the laboratory (Sexual Alchemy); thus, this is how the serpent moves about and is joyful. Chant I.A.O. seven times while in the laboratorium oratorium.

The mantra I.N.R.I. has an absolute power over the fire; chant this mantra also in the laboratorium oratorium in order to carry the fire to each one of your seven chakras. Chant I.N.R.I as follows:

INRI ENRE ONRO UNRU ANRA. These mantras must be chanted by syllabifying them as follows:

> **Iiinnn Rrriii** (clairvoyance)
> **Eeennn Rrreee** (clairaudience)
> **Ooonnn Rrrooo** (heart – intuition)
> **Uuunnn Rrruuu** (telepathy –solar plexus)
> **Aaannn Rrraaa** (pulmonary chakras – memory of past lives)

The great Hierophant Jesus Christ chanted these mantras in the laboratorium oratorium of the pyramid of Kephren.

The seven kabbalistic signs of the planets are:

Moon: A globe divided by two middle moons.

---

68 The three voices that sing in *Atalanta fugiens*. See Atalanta in the glossary.

Mercury: A caduceus and the cynocephalus.

Venus: A sexual lingam.

Sun: A serpent with the head of a lion.

Mars: A dragon biting a sword's guard.

Jupiter: A pentagram, or an eagle's beak.

Saturn: A limping elder, or a rock entwined by a serpent.

The seven talismans have the power of attracting the seven planetary forces. Gold is the metal of the Sun. Silver is the metal of the Moon. Iron is the metal of Mars. Copper is the metal of Venus. Quicksilver is the metal of Mercury. Tin is the metal of Jupiter, and lead is the metal of Saturn. Perfect talismans can be prepared with the proper stones and metals.

The Pater Noster (Lord's Prayer) is the most perfect prayer because it has seven magical petitions.[69]

Practice

Asana:[70] student, you must lie down on the floor so that you can spread out your arms and legs to each side until you form the five-pointed star. Relax your whole body. Do not think about anything, empty your mind. Concentrate your mind on your Inner God, and start praying the Pater Noster extremely slowly, and think about the sense of each petition. Become sleepy, fall profoundly asleep while meditating upon each word, upon each phrase, worshiping... worshiping... worshiping...

Student, you must not move when you wake up... be motionless and practice a retrospective exercise in order to remember your internal experiences: remember where you were, what places you visited while in the astral body, what you did, what you saw, etc. This practice must be performed daily without ever becoming weary. Seeing and hearing the great internal realities must be your goal.

---

69 See glossary.

70 Sanskrit, posture.

THE EIGHTH KEY OF BASIL VALENTINE, FROM VIRIDARIUM CHYMICUM, 1624

Arcanum 8

Let us study in this lecture the Eighth Key of Basil Valentine, an illustration of the *Viridarium Chymicum*.

The Eighth Key is a clear and perfect alchemical allegory of the processes of death and resurrection that inevitably occur in the esoteric preparation of the Philosophical Stone.

The entire inner preparation of the stone and the metallic transmutation are represented in this allegory. The entire human material employed in this work dies, it becomes rotten, corrupted and becomes blackened within the philosophical egg, then it becomes marvelously white.

The entire work of the Great Work is found within the philosophical egg. The masculine and feminine sexual principles are contained within the egg. Thus, like the fledgling that emerges from the egg, or like the universe of Brahma that emerges from the golden egg, so too does the master emerge from the philosophical egg.

The Eighth Key, an illustration of the *Viridarium Chymicum*, shows death represented as a corpse, putrefaction represented as crows, sowing as a humble agriculturalist, growth as a wheat stalk, and resurrection by a deceased person who rises from the grave and by an angel that plays the trumpet of the Final Judgment.

We, the Gnostics, know that in the Eighth Key the corpse, death, represents the two witnesses of the Apocalypse (Revelation 11: 3-6) that are now dead. By means of alchemical putrefaction, by means of the works of alchemy (represented by the crows), the two witnesses resurrect.

Our motto is Thelema. The entire power is found enclosed within the seed that is symbolized in the wheat stalk. The sacred angel that we carry within plays his trumpet, and the two witnesses rise from the grave.

Two archers, one who hit the bull's eye and the other who misses, symbolize the two alchemical interpretations that can occur, the right and the wrong: white sexual magic and black sexual magic, golden alchemy and satanic eroticism.

There is no ejaculation of the ens seminis in golden alchemy, whereas in satanic eroticism there is ejaculation of the ens seminis. In India, the black yogis (asura samphata) ejaculate the ens seminis (शुक्र shukra) in order to criminally mix it with the feminine रजस् rajas[71] within the vagina, thereafter; by handling the "vajroli"[72] in a negative way, they reabsorb this fluid that was mixed with feminine rajas. The black yogis (drukpas)[73] believe that through this way they are wisely achieving the union of the solar and lunar atoms in order to awaken the Kundalini, but the outcome of such black tantra is the negative awakening of the serpent (Kundabuffer). Therefore instead of ascending, the serpent descends downwards into the atomic infernos of the human being and becomes the tail of Satan.

This is how these black yogis end up separating themselves from their inner god forever; they become demons. So, that is black magic. Through this way the two witnesses of the Apocalypse do not ever resurrect because this way leads into the abyss and the second death. Therefore, whosoever ejaculates his seminal liquor withdraws himself from his inner god.

The yogis who practice Oordhavareta Yoga (positive Sexual Magic) do not ejaculate their ens seminis. Through this way, the combination of shukra (solar atoms) and rajas (lunar atoms) is performed within the philosophical egg, in other words, within the very sexual laboratory of the alchemist.

Thus, this is how the two witnesses[74] resurrect.

> *"These are the two olive trees, and the two candlesticks standing before the God of the earth. And if any man will hurt them, fire proceed out of their mouth, and devour their enemies: and if any man will hurt them, he must in this manner be killed. These have power to*

---

71 Has many meanings, but two are evoked here: in black tantra, the impure aspect of rajas is utilized, which relates to menstrual discharge. In white tantra, rajas refers to the feminine aspect of semen (seed), the sexual energy either in women or in the lunar channel along the spine.

72 A method of handling the sexual forces, which in this case is negative.

73 "Dragons," which can be pure or impure.

74 "And I will give power unto my two witnesses, and they shall prophesy..." —Revelation 11:3

*shut heaven (to those who practice Sexual Magic with
seminal ejaculation), that it rain not in the days of their
prophecy: and have power over (the human) waters
to turn them to blood, and to smite the (philosophical)
earth (the human organism of fornicators) with all
plagues, as often as they will (according with the law)."*
—Revelation 11:4-6

Disposition of the Two Witnesses

The two witnesses are a semi-ethereal,
semi-physical pair of sympathetic cords
that are entwined along the spinal medulla,
forming the Caduceus of Mercury, the sacred
eight, the sign of the infinite. In the male, the
two witnesses part from the right and left testi-
cles and in the female they part from the ovaries.
These two witnesses are situated to the right and
left sides of the dorsal spine. The two witnesses alternatively
ascend from left to right until forming a marvelous knot in
that space situated between the two eyebrows, thereafter they
continue through the nasal cavities. The two witnesses connect
the sexual organs with the nasal cavities. The ganglionic cord
that proceeds from the left side is cold, lunar and the ganglionic cord that proceeds from the right side is hot, solar.[75]
These two nervous cords are graciously knotted in the coccyx.
The Kundalini (serpent of brass, nachash) awakens when the
solar and lunar atoms of the seminal system make contact in
the Triveni, close to the coccyx.

The sexual act between the male and female initiates has
only one objective, that of establishing a contact of opposite
poles in order to awaken their Kundalini; because the mercury
of secret philosophy is multiplied (the seminal fluid increases)
with the sexual contact and when the ens seminis is not ejacu-
lated it is transmuted into seminal vapors. These vapors, in its
turn, are converted, are bipolarized into positive and negative

---

75   In the male, the lunar rises from the right testicle and the solar from the
left testicle. In the female, they are reversed.

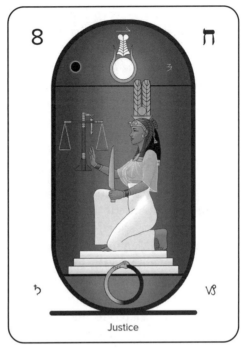

Justice

ARCANUM 8

energies. The positive are solar forces, the negative are lunar forces; these solar and lunar energies rise through the pair of sympathetic cords that are known as the two witnesses: Ida and Pingala.

The medullar canal has an inner orifice that is normally found blocked in ordinary people; however the seminal vapors open up this orifice so that the sacred serpent (of brass, nachash) can enter there within that medullar canal.

It is necessary to warn the Gnostic-Rosicrucian brothers and sisters that they must learn how to polarize the sacred fire of the Kundalini. Some devotees eat meat everyday and drink alcohol; with the pretext of working in the Great Work they pleasurably enjoy lust, they bestially enjoy carnal passion, even when they do not waste their ens seminis. Therefore, the outcome of this is that these devotees totally polarize the fire within the chakras of their lower abdomen and lose the happiness of enjoying the ecstasy of the lotus of one thousand petals. That lotus flower is situated in the pineal gland, which is the crown of saints that shines over the head of the great initiates. The lotus of one thousand petals converts us into masters of samadhi (ecstasy).

The work in the laboratorium oratorium is a true mystical ceremony that must not be profaned by animal desire or by sinful thoughts. Sex is the sanctum regnum of the temple, therefore, purify your mind from any type of impure thoughts when entering in the sanctum of sanctums.

Esoteric Ordeals

The Eighth Arcanum encloses the initiatic ordeals. Each initiation, each degree, has its ordeals. These initiatic ordeals get stricter each time, in accordance with the initiatic degree. The number 8 is the degree of Job.[76] This sign, this number, signifies ordeals and sufferings. These initiatic ordeals are performed in the superior worlds and in the physical world.

A woman with a sword in her hand, facing the scale of cosmic justice appears in the Eighth Arcanum of the Tarot. Indeed, only she (the priestess) can deliver the sword to the magician, thus, an initiate (the priest) without a woman cannot receive the sword.

There is Eve-Venus, the instinctual woman; Venus-Eve, the noble woman of the home. There is also Venus-Urania, the woman initiated into the great mysteries, and finally, we confirm the existence of Urania-Venus, the female adept, the woman who is Self-realized in depth.

The Flaming Fire

The flaming fire opens the seven churches of the Apocalypse (seven magnetic centers of the spinal medulla).

We conquer the powers of the earth with the first center (situated at the height of the sexual organs).

We conquer the water with the second center (situated at the height of the prostate/uterus).

---

76 In the Tanakh / Bible, Job was severely tested by Lucifer.

We conquer the universal fire with the third center (situated at the height of the navel).

We conquer the air with the fourth center (situated at the height of the heart); the heart is the sanctuary of Sephirah, the Mother of the Sephiroth, the Divine Cosmic Mother.

With the fifth center (situated at the height of the larynx) we receive the sacred ear and dominate the Akasha with which we can preserve the physical body alive (even during the great cosmic nights).

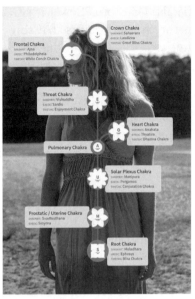

SEVEN PRIMARY CHAKRAS AND CHURCHES

We conquer the magnetic center of the Father with the sixth center (situated between the two eyebrows), thus we become clairvoyant.

We receive the polyvoyance, the intuitive sight, the ecstasy, with the seventh center (situated in the pineal gland).

The Equilibrium of the Scale

The woman of the Eighth Arcanum of the Tarot has in one hand the scale, and in the other, the sword. It is necessary to equilibrate the forces; it is necessary and urgent to completely sanctify ourselves and to practice the Arcanum A.Z.F. The forces of man and woman are equilibrated with love and with wisdom.

Venus equilibrates the works of Mars.

Mercury equilibrates and performs the works of the Sun and of the Moon, above in the Macrocosmos and below in the Microcosmic human being.

The works of the Sun and of the Moon, the man and the woman are equilibrated by the Mercury of the secret philosophy (the ens seminis).

Old Saturn balances thundering Jupiter, the father of all gods. This is the law of equilibrium.

A yogi (or a yogini) cannot Self-realize himself without the Arcanum A.Z.F., therefore those who want to exclude the Arcanum A.Z.F. from their whole yoga are violating the law of the Eighth Arcanum. They are failures.

The double cross on the wheel of Pythagoras and on the wheel of Ezekiel are pantacles that represent the Eighth Arcanum.

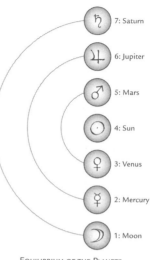

7: Saturn
6: Jupiter
5: Mars
4: Sun
3: Venus
2: Mercury
1: Moon

EQUILIBRIUM OF THE PLANETS

IX. CLAVIS.

THE NINTH KEY OF BASIL VALENTINE

Arcanum 9

The Ninth Key represents old Saturn falling and the Goddess Moon victoriously rising. Saturn is the lead and the Moon is the silver. The terrestrial Adam,[77] the psychological "I" must fall and die so that the Adam-Christ can be born within us. We need to transmute the lead into gold. The lead of our personality must be transmuted into the gold of the Spirit.

The Moon-Mercury-Sophic (the ens seminis) must rise and return inwardly and upwardly.

To disincarnate signifies to perpetuate error. The psychological "I," the terrestrial Adam, is born millions of times; it incarnates in order to satisfy desires. Terrestrial births are the perpetuation of ignorance. To be born in spirit and in truth signifies death for the terrestrial Adam.

The Adam-Christ is born from the seed. The grain, the seed, needs Thelema (willpower) in order for the superhuman to heroically germinate; the birth of the superhuman is not the outcome of evolution. The superhuman does not need to evolve to attain perfection as is assumed by many students of esotericism. Evolution is simply the movement of the universal life according to the concepts of time, space, and movement. All possibilities are contained within the evolving nature; thus, many become very good and others very bad. Nonetheless, the superhuman is not the result of any sort of evolution but the outcome of a tremendous revolution of the consciousness.

Adam-Christ is as different from the terrestrial Adam as lightning is from a black cloud. Lightning is born from a cloud, yet it is not a cloud. Lightning is like the superhuman while the cloud is like the man. To be born is a sexual problem, the path is sexual transmutation.

A rectangle appears in the Ninth Key, this represents the four elements of Alchemy. By carefully studying this rectangle, we discover a double circle that wisely symbolizes the mercu-

---

77 (Hebrew אדם) Literally, "The first." In the Judeo-Christian tradition, the name of the first human being. The name Adam actually has many esoteric meanings that are unknown to the public.

rial matter with its two properties (generation and regeneration). The double circle contains three serpents that emerge from three hearts. Indeed, we need to work with Mercury, Sulfur, and Salt in order to lift the metallic serpent upon the pole. The Adam-Christ is born in us only by working with the prima matter: Mercury, Sulfur, and Salt; the Phoenix Bird that is born from its own ashes stands upon the double circle of Mercurial matter. We need to become imitators of this mythological bird; however, this is only possible when we work with the seed.

The eagle of volatility is the terrestrial Adam dominated by the crow of putrefaction. The goddess Moon carries a white swan upon her head. We must whiten the crow with sexual transmutation until transforming it into the immaculate swan of Ascension.

The entire symbolism of the Great Work is enclosed within the Ninth Key. No one can work with the sephirothic tree without being an alchemist and a kabbalist. The wise one of the Ninth Arcanum must search for the treasury within the Ninth Sphere. It is necessary to study the explanatory statements, the principles and methods of the science of Kabbalah and to work with the seed.

"Practice cannot exist without theory."

The Ninth Sphere

An esotericist sentence affirms that "One can only depart through the same door that one entered." We departed from Eden. Eden is sex itself. Therefore, only through the doors of sex can we enter into Eden. The fetus (after having accomplished its entire process of gestation) arrives at the moment when it must depart through the same door that its seed-germ entered. This is the law.

The physical body of the human being is the outcome of nine months of gestation within the maternal womb. By means of philosophical analogies we also deduce that the human species remained within the maternal womb of the Divine Cosmic Mother Isis (Rhea, Cybele, Mary, Adonia,

Insobertha, Kali, etc.) gestating for nine ages.

In the "authentic initiation," this return to the point of departure is nothing more than the descent into the Ninth Sphere, which is a test of action for the supreme dignity of the great hierophant of mysteries.

The flaming forge of Vulcan is found in the Ninth Sphere (sex). There, Mars descends in order to retemper his flaming sword and conquer the heart of Venus (the Venustic Initiation[78]). Hercules descends in order to clean the stables of Augias (our animal depths). Perseus descends in order to cut off the head of Medusa (the psychological "I," or the terrestrial Adam) with his flaming sword.

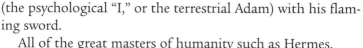

יסוד
Yesod:
"foundation" (of life)

THE NINTH SPHERE

All of the great masters of humanity such as Hermes, Buddha, Jesus, Dante, Zoroaster, etc., had to pass through this utmost test. The following phrase is written upon the frightful threshold of the Ninth Sphere (which does not grant access to profaners): "Lasciate ogni speranza voi ch'entrate" (Abandon hope, all you who enter here).[79]

The Zohar emphatically warns us that within the depths of the abyss lives the Adam protoplastus,[80] the differentiating principle of the souls. With this principle we have to dispute victory to the death. This fight is terrible, brain against sex, and sex against brain, and what is even more terrible and more painful is heart against heart, you know this.

Resplendently, the sign of the infinite is within the heart of the Earth. The sign of the infinite is the Holy Eight.

---

78   See glossary.
79   From Dante's Inferno.
80   Protoplast, from ancient Greek πρωτόπλαστος, "first formed."

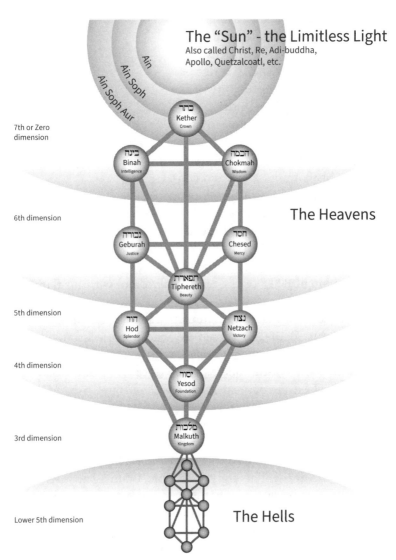

The "Sun" - the Limitless Light
Also called Christ, Re, Adi-buddha, Apollo, Quetzalcoatl, etc.

Ain
Ain Soph
Ain Soph Aur

7th or Zero dimension

כתר
Kether
Crown

בינה
Binah
Intelligence

חכמה
Chokmah
Wisdom

6th dimension

The Heavens

גבורה
Geburah
Justice

חסד
Chesed
Mercy

תפארת
Tiphereth
Beauty

5th dimension

הוד
Hod
Splendor

נצח
Netzach
Victory

4th dimension

יסוד
Yesod
Foundation

מלכות
Malkuth
Kingdom

3rd dimension

Lower 5th dimension

The Hells

HELLS ON THE TREE OF LIFE

In Kabbalah, the hells are nine spheres within the "Earth" (Malkuth) that mirror the worlds above. They hells are called klipoth ("empty shells") because the souls who descend into the inferior worlds lose connection to their own inner divinity, therefore they are "empty shells."

In this sign the heart, brain, and sex of the genie of the earth are represented. The secret name of this genie is Cham-Gam.

The sign of the infinite is in the center of the Ninth Sphere. The earth has nine atomic strata and the sign of the infinite is found within the ninth stratum. The nine Initiations of Minor Mysteries gradually corresponds with each one of these nine strata. Each Initiation of Minor Mysteries gives access to each one of these terrestrial strata. Therefore, only the ones who have attained the nine Initiations of Minor Mysteries can reach the heart of the earth.

Each terrestrial stratum is guarded by terrifying guardians. Secret paths lead the disciple towards the heart of the Earth. The double vital current of the genie of the Earth is represented in the sign of the infinite.

The double vital current sustains and nourishes the entire planet Earth, thus, we (all the living beings) are organized upon this divine archetype.

There is a divine atom in the center of the sign of the infinite. The nine spheres of atomic vibration are concentrically focused within this atom of the genie of the Earth.

The Holy Eight is resplendent with glory within the center of the Earth. In the center of this Holy Eight the central atom is found, which is where the nine spheres of universal vibration are focused; this is the law.

Kabbalistic Traditions

Kabbalistic traditions tell us that Adam had two wives, Lilith[81] and Nahemah.[82] It is stated that Lilith is the mother of abortion, homosexuality and all crimes against nature in general. Nahemah is the malignant and fatal beauty. Nahemah is the mother of adultery and passionate fornication.

Any marriage that is a violation of the law is easy to recognize because on the day of the wedding, the bride appears bald. Since hair is the symbol of chastity for the woman, on

---

81 See glossary.
82 See glossary.

LILITH לילית, "THE NIGHT VISITOR"

wedding days of Nahemah it is prohibited to display hair, thus she instinctively covers her hair with the veil (as if she is trying to conceal it).

Thus, the abyss is divided into two large infrasexual[83] spheres. These are the spheres of Lilith and Nahemah. The inhabitants of the sphere of Lilith do not have any hope for salvation, whereas the inhabitants of the sphere of Nahemah still have hope for redemption.

Sphere of Lilith

Here we find those who abhor sex, for example, monks, anchorites, mystics, spiritualists, people from different pseudo-esoteric organizations, etc. All types of infrasexual people hate sex and consider themselves to be highly superior to those of

---

83   Inferior sexuality; ie. incapable of creation.

normal sexuality. All of the taboos, restrictions, and prejudices that currently condition the lives of people of normal sexuality were firmly established by infrasexual people. Infrasexual people mortally hate the Arcanum A.Z.F. nevertheless, they give to themselves special credentials, and therefore, it is not difficult to find homosexuality within many convents and schools that are dedicated to spiritualistic or pseudo-esoteric studies. All of the crimes against nature are found in the infrasexual sphere of Lilith.

Sphere of Nahemah

Nahemah seduces with the enchantment of her malignant beauty. Adultery is the outcome of this fatal enchantment. In the sphere of Nahemah we find the delectable cruelties from the kingdom of infrasexuality. In the atomic regions of the infrasexual sphere of Nahemah live the Don Giovanni types of men and Dona Ines or rather the beautiful hetairai,[84] sometimes sweet and sometimes cruel in others. If people of normal sexuality do not live alert and vigilant, they can convert themselves into fatal proselytes of these infrasexual people, since they garnish themselves as saints, apostles, anchorites, etc. and believe themselves to be superior; they go and cheat the people of normal sexuality, converting them into their henchmen.

Understand that people of normal sexuality[85] are those who have no sexual conflicts of any kind. The sexual force of the people of normal sexuality is in perfect equilibrium with the spheres of thought, feeling, and will. These types of people do not abuse sex nor do they have any type of sexual aberrations.

The sphere of suprasexuality[86] is the sphere of internal illumination.

---

84 Greek, a courtesan, whether chaste and pure or fallen into prostitution.
85 "Normal sexuality results from total harmony and concordance with all the other functions. Normal sexuality bestows upon us the power to create healthy children, to create in the world of art or the sciences. Any negative mental attitude towards sex produces infiltration of this powerful energy into other functions, which provokes frightening catastrophes, fatally resulting in infrasexuality." —Samael Aun Weor, *The Perfect Matrimony*
86 Superior sexuality, capable of creating superior results.

Sexual enjoyment precedes mystical ecstasy. Sexual sensations are transmuted into sensations of ineffable ecstasy. The human life span of mystical ecstasy is always preceded by the human life span of sexual enjoyment. Thus, the human life span of mystical ecstasy begins where the human life span of sexual enjoyment ends.

After having attained the Venustic Initiation—in other words, after the Adam-Christ has been born within us—we must then extract the philosophical egg from the rottenness of the matter and deliver it to the Son of Man,[87] meaning to transplant the totality of the sexual energies to Adam-Christ; this is how he becomes absolutely strong.

The path is named transmutation and sexual sublimation. Whosoever reaches these heights becomes a master of samadhi.

The same energy that produces sexual sensations (when it is transmuted) then produces mystical ecstasy.

Christ, Buddha, Hermes, Quetzalcoatl, and many other avatars were suprasexual.

The Forge of Vulcan

Sexual energy is divided into three distinct types.

First: the energy having to do with the reproduction of the species.

Second: the energy having to do with the spheres of thought, feeling, and will.

Third: the energy that is found related with the world of pure Spirit.

All of the processes related with sexual transmutation are possible because of the intermediation of the vital body.[88] This is the Archaeus[89] that elaborates the blood and the semen

---

87 See glossary.
88 See glossary.
89 In alchemy, archeus refers to the vital principle or force that presides over the growth and continuation of living beings; the anima mundi or malleable power of the alchemists and philosophers.

in the human organism. This is Vulcan[90] that transmutes
the seminal liquor into Christic energy. The vital body is the
vehicle of the soul consciousness in the human being. The consciousness is the flame, and the vital body is the wick. Vulcan
exists within the Microcosmos and within the Macrocosmos,
in the human being and in Nature. The great Vulcan of Nature
is Eden, the ethereal plane.

Cosmic Rhythms

Any alchemist fledgling (after having been crowned) is leaving the sexual act little by little; the secret connubial becomes
more and more distant according to certain cosmic rhythms
marked by the oriental gong. This is how the sexual energies
are sublimated and transmuted in a continuous ecstasy.

The alchemist fledgling that worked in the magisterium of
fire in former reincarnations performs this laboratory work in
a relatively short time. However, those who for the first time
work in the Great Work need at least twenty years of intense
work in order to enter into the second part, for another twenty
years in order to slowly withdraw from the work of the laboratory; a total of forty years in order to perform the entire work.
However, when the alchemist spills the cup of Hermes, the fire
of the furnace of his laboratory is extinguished and the entire
work is lost.

Mantras for Sexual Magic

I.A.O. OU AOAI OUO OUOAE KORE

Now continue with the powerful mantras:

Kawlakaw, Sawlasaw, Zeesar

Kawlakaw is the inner God. **Sawlasaw** is the terrestrial
man, and **Zeesar** is the astral body. These powerful mantras
develop all of the internal powers. We have already mentioned

90   The Latin or Roman name for the Greek god Ἥφαιστος Hephaestus,
    known by the Egyptians as Ptah. A god of fire with a deep and ancient
    mythology, commonly remembered as the blacksmith who forges weap-
    ons for gods and heroes.

ARCANUM 9

the mantra INRI and its modifications. The alchemist must not forget any of these mantras.

The Ninth Arcanum of the Tarot is the prudent and wise hermit who is covered with the protective robe of Apollonius, which symbolizes prudence; he holds onto the staff of the patriarchs, and illuminates himself with the lamp of Hermes (wisdom).

The alchemist must always perform the will of the Father.

One must be humble in order to attain wisdom, and after having attained it, one must be even more humble, more than anyone else.

It is better to be silent and die.

While the sinning Adam is dying, the Adam-Christ is sequentially being born.

10

Retribution

ARCANUM 10

Arcanum 10

In this lecture we are going to study the Arcanum 10 of the Tarot. It is necessary to analyze the cosmogonic wheel of Ezekiel.[91] In this wheel, we find the battle of antitheses. Hermanubis[92] rises on the right and Typhon[93] descends through the left of the fatal wheel. This is the wheel of the centuries, the wheel of reincarnations and of karma. Upon the wheel appears the mystery of the sphinx grasps the flaming sword between its lion's paws. This is the wheel of antitheses. The serpent of brass that healed the Israelites in the wilderness

91 Read the book of Ezekiel in the Tanakh / Bible.
92 Greek Hermes + Egyptian Anubis. A name that first appeared in Roman Egypt to symbolize the revealer of mysteries of the lower world, not of hell or hades, but of our Earth (the lowest world in the chain of worlds), and also of the sexual mysteries.
93 The adversary of Osiris, representative of declining, devolving forces.

and the terrible, tempting serpent of Eden are fighting each other.

The entire secret of the Tree of Knowledge[94] is enclosed within this wheel; the four rivers of paradise[95] flow from this unique fountain, one of them runs through the thick sunny jungle watering the philosophical earth of gold and light and the other tenebrously and turbulently runs into the kingdom of the Abyss. Light and darkness, white magic and black magic, are fighting each other. Eros and Anteros,[96] Cain and Abel,[97] live within us in an intense battle, until by discovering the mystery of the sphinx, we grasp the flaming sword, and thus, this is how we become liberated from the wheel of the centuries.

Lunar Conscience

The lunar conscience is the outcome of our unfaithful memory; this type of consciousness sleeps profoundly. The humanoid is conscious of what he remembers; no humanoid is conscious of what he does not remember. The sinning Adam is memory, he is the reincarnating ego, he is the lunar is conscious. Clairvoyants affirm that the atoms of the secret enemy[98] constitute this is consciousness, and that it is a tenebrous remnant of our lunar past (a threshold's larva).

Our Gnostic disciples must comprehend the significance of this type of consciousness: the lunar consciousness is something that must become conscious; and it needs someone who is conscious of it. The lunar consciousness is submitted to every type of limitation, qualification, restriction, reaction; it is the outcome of matter, the outcome of our race's inheritance, family, habits, customs, prejudices, desires, fears, appetencies, etc.

The sinning Adam with its lunar consciousness reincarnates with the goal of gaining more experiences within the school

---

94 See glossary.
95 As described in Genesis 2, and explained in *The Revolution of Beelzebub*.
96 Greek equivilent of Christ and Antichrist.
97 Brothers described by Moses in Bereshit / Genesis.
98 See glossary.

of life. However, life's experiences complicate and strengthen the sinning Adam. The once innocent humanity from Eden is now this terrible and perverse humanity of the atomic and hydrogen bomb.

The innocent child (with the experiences of life) is converted into a sly, distrustful, malicious, avaricious, fearful elder; such is the lunar conscience. The devil is a devil and can never acquire perfection. The great Master H.P. Blavatsky stated:

> *"Make hard thy Soul against the snares of Self ["I"]; deserve for it the name of "Diamond-Soul."*
> —The Voice of the Silence

Solar Conscience

There are changes in the lunar consciousness, and there are changes of consciousness. Every improvement in the lunar conscience originates changes within it. These types of changes in the lunar conscience are superficial and useless. What we need is a change of consciousness. When we dissolve the lunar consciousness then the solar consciousness is born within us.

It is necessary for the sinning Adam to die within us so that Adam-Christ can be born within us. We grasp the flaming sword when we liberate the solar electronic energy that is enclosed within the seminal atoms.

Perseus descends into the flaming forge of Vulcan in order to decapitate the sinning Adam (Medusa) with his flaming sword. John the Baptist is decapitated and Christ is crucified in order to save the world. The slaughter of the innocent children (the initiates) is a repetitive action throughout the initiation. This is how the solar consciousness is born within us. This type of consciousness contains in itself knower, knowledge, and the known thing: three in one and one in three.

Solar consciousness is omnipresent and omnipenetrating. Solar consciousness liberates the human being from the fatal wheel of the centuries.

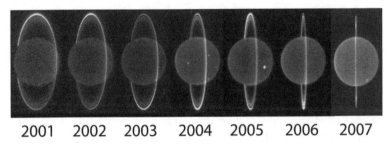

2001   2002   2003   2004   2005   2006   2007

URANUS PHOTOGRAPHED BY NASA

Sexual Cycles

Uranus is the octave of Venus. It governs the masculine and feminine facets of sex. It has a sexual cycle of eighty-four years. Uranus's cycle is divided into two periods of 42 years: positive (+) masculine, and negative (-) feminine. Uranus' two poles are always facing toward the sun. For 42 years the positive pole is directed towards the sun and another 42 years the negative pole. Now we can understand where that alternating stimuli for the sexes comes from; the marvelous biorhythm of 84 years. The wheel of the centuries rotates in periods of forty-two years each. The masculine sex predominates for one half and the feminine sex for the other half.

The sexual cycle of Uranus corresponds with the average length of a human life; this signifies that the antithesis of the sexual cycle in which we were born vibrates within us during our adulthood. Then we feel sexually stimulated. We comprehend why mature men and women are indeed mature enough to work in the Great Work, because sexual sentiments are more vigorous at forty years of age.

Light and Consciousness

Light and consciousness are two phenomena of the same thing. The more levels of Christic consciousness we develop, the more levels of light we attain.

The planets are gradually absorbing the Christic consciousness of the Sun. Thus when the planets of our solar system have integrally absorbed the divine solar consciousness, then life, light, and heat will no longer occupy only the astronomical place of the Sun, but the entire solar system will shine like the Sun. This is the case of the gigantic sun Antares, which is a million times more rarified than our Sun. The light of the solar system of Antares is not only localized in its sun, because each one of its planets has become a sun. The planetary humanities enjoy the solar consciousness; the outcome of this joy is the splendors of the solar system of Antares.

The Ten Sephiroth

Ten sephiroth are spoken of, but in reality, there are twelve. The Ain Soph is the eleventh, and the twelfth sephirah is its tenebrous antithesis within the abyss.

These are twelve spheres or universal regions, which interpenetrate each other without confusion. These twelve spheres gravitate within the central atom of the sign of the infinite. A solar humanity unfolds within these twelve spheres.

We have said that the sign of the infinite is in the center of the earth, in the heart of the earth. The ten sephiroth of universal vibration emanate from the Ain Soph (the microcosmic star) that guides our interior. The Ain Soph is the Being of our Being.

The ten sephiroth emanate from the Ain Soph as follows:

First, Kether כתר, the Ancient of Days

Second, Chokmah חכמה, the region of wisdom

Third, Binah בינה, intelligence

Fourth, Chesed חסד, the world of the Innermost

Fifth, Geburah גבורה, the world of soul-consciousness, the region of rigor and justice

Sixth, Tiphereth תפארת, the causal world, the region of willpower, equilibrium, and beauty

Seventh, Netzach נצח, the region of victory, the world of the mental human (anyone who liberates himself from the four bodies of sin is a Buddha)[99].

Eighth, Hod הוד, the splendor, the region of the astral body

99 The term buddha is an honorific that means "awakened."

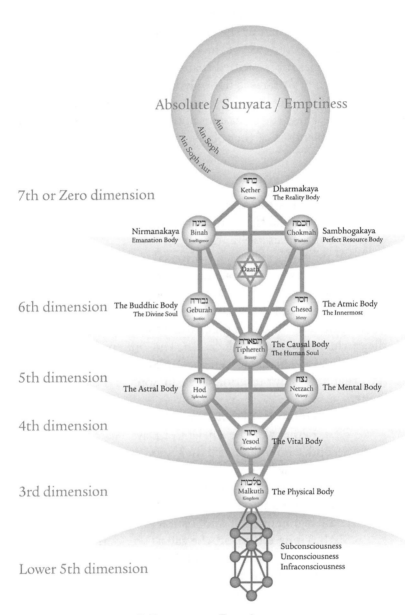

Absolute / Sunyata / Emptiness

Ain
Ain Soph
Ain Soph Aur

7th or Zero dimension

כתר
Kether
Crown
Dharmakaya
The Reality Body

Nirmanakaya
Emanation Body

בינה
Binah
Intelligence

חכמה
Chokmah
Wisdom

Sambhogakaya
Perfect Resource Body

Daath

6th dimension

The Buddhic Body
The Divine Soul

גבורה
Geburah
Justice

חסד
Chesed
Mercy

The Atmic Body
The Innermost

הפארת
Tiphereth
Beauty

The Causal Body
The Human Soul

5th dimension

The Astral Body

הוד
Hod
Splendor

נצח
Netzach
Victory

The Mental Body

4th dimension

יסוד
Yesod
Foundation

The Vital Body

3rd dimension

מלכות
Malkuth
Kingdom

The Physical Body

Lower 5th dimension

Subconsciousness
Unconsciousness
Infraconsciousness

THE SEPHIROTH OF THE TREE OF LIFE

Ninth, Yesod יסוד, foundation, sex, the ethereal plane

Tenth, Malkuth מלכות, the kingdom in general, the
physical world; Malkuth is a supreme filter; from this
region we depart to the Ain Soph or to the abyss, such
is the law.

The sephiroth are atomic; these ten sephiroth can be
reduced to three tables:

First: the quantum table of the radiant energy that
comes from the Sun

Second: the atomic weight table of the elements of
Nature

Third: the molecular weight table of the compounds

This is Jacob's ladder, which goes from earth to heaven. All
of the worlds of cosmic consciousness are reduced to these
three tables.

All of the ten known sephiroth come from Sephirah, the
Divine Mother. She dwells in the heart temple.

Direct Clue for Direct Knowledge

It is necessary that our Gnostic disciples learn how to
leave their physical body in order to travel with their internal
vehicles with complete cognizance in order to penetrate within
the distinct sephirothic regions.

It is necessary to directly know the twelve spheres of universal vibration, where all of the beings of the universe develop
and live. The disciple must concentrate on the chakra of the
heart, which is where the Divine Cosmic Mother abides. The
disciple must beseech Sephirah, the mother of the sephiroth.
The disciple muse beg her to take one out of the physical body
to the distinct departments of the kingdom in order to directly
study the sephiroth of Kabbalah. The disciple must pray and
meditate abundantly on the Divine Mother while mentally
vocalizing the following kabbalistic mantras:

Lifaros – Lifaros – Licanto – Ligoria

Vocalize these mantras by syllabifying them. If you carefully
observe the intelligent phonetic structure of these mantras,
you will see the three vowels I.A.O. of the great mysteries.

I.A.O. is hidden and combined in these sacred mantras of Kabbalah. The disciple must become sleepy while mentally vocalizing these four kabbalistic mantras.

It is necessary to practice a retrospective exercise when awakening from our normal sleep in order to remember what we have seen and heard during the dream.

Initiation

Flee from those who sell initiations. Remember that initiation is your own life. If you want initiation, write it upon a reed (whosoever understands this let him understand it, for there is wisdom within).

The path of liberation is represented by the life, passion, death, resurrection, and ascension of our beloved savior.[100]

Remember that your ego does not receive initiations. Thus, you must not boast of being an initiate; do not say, "I have these initiations" or "I have these powers" because this is arrogance and vanity. Only the Innermost receives initiations. You, wretched creature, are nothing but the sinning shadow of the one who has never sinned. Exert yourself so that you can die more and more within yourself so that the Son of Man can be born within you.

---

100 Study the four gospels of the Christian Bible.

Persuasion

ARCANUM 11

Arcanum 11

The study of the Eleventh Arcanum of the Tarot corresponds to this lecture. The hieroglyphic of this arcanum is a beautiful woman crowned with the sacred sign of infinity and who very gently (with Olympic serenity) shuts the jaw of a furious lion[101] with her own hands.

Divine kings' thrones were adorned with lions made out of massive amounts of gold. The gold signifies the sacred fire of Kundalini; this reminds us of Horus, oro (Spanish for gold). We need to transmute the lead of the personality into the gold of the Spirit and only in the alchemist's laboratorium is it possible to perform this work.

---

101 "The lion is the element fire and also represents gold." —Samael Aun
Weor, *Tarot and Kabbalah*

MITHRAS, ZOROASTRIAN SYMBOL OF CHRIST

Mithras

When the alchemist fledgling is crowned, he is transformed into a god of fire; it is then that he opens the terrible jaws of the furious lion with his own hands.

The potable gold[102] of alchemy is the sacred fire of the Holy Spirit. To bind the cross / human within the triangle / spirit would be impossible without the potable gold.

SULFUR = FIRE

The Number 11

The number 11 is formed by two unities (1) that Heinrich Kunrath translated in these two words, "Coagula Solve."[103]

We need to accumulate the sacred fire, and then learn to project it. The clue to this is in the connection of the

---

102 Read *Treatise of Sexual Alchemy* by Samael Aun Weor.
103 Latin for the opposing and complementary processes of alchemy: dissolution and coagulation.

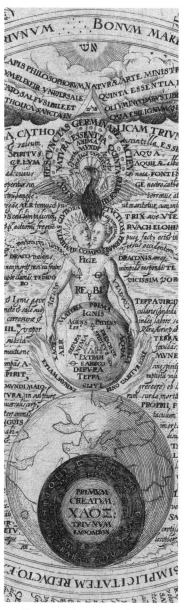

DETAIL FROM *AMPHITHEATRUM SAPIENTIAE AETERNAE* (1602) BY HEINRICH KHUNRATH

The words Coagula and Solve are written on the arms of the conjoined man and woman (the "11").

membrum virile[104] with the genitalia murielis,[105] quietude of the membrum virile and the genitalia murielis, and the use of a very gentle movement occasionally. Thus, we transmute the animal instincts into willpower, the sexual passion into love, lustful thoughts into comprehension, and vocalize the secret mantras.

The number eleven is kabbalistically disarranged as follows: 1 plus 1 equals 2. Number 1 is masculine and number 2 is feminine.

The Pairs of Opposites of Holy Alchemy

Positive • Negative
Active • Passive
Osiris • Isis
Baal / Bel • Astarte / Ishtar
Shiva • Parvati
Husband • Wife
Father • Mother
Sun • Moon
Fire • Water
Heat • Cold
Volatile • Fixed
Sulfur • Mercury

---

104 Latin euphamism for the male sexual organ.
105 Latin euphamism for the female sexual organ.

Chinese Alchemy

Heaven is masculine, yáng, and its element is fire. The earth is feminine, yīn, and its element is water.

In the Taoist doctrine, we find White Tantra. Yīnyáng,[106] the dragon and the tiger, are the axis of

阴阳 YĪNYÁNG

Taoism. According to Taoist interpretation, Yīnyáng is the outcome of Taiji,[107] the prima matter of the universe, and creation emerges from the sexual union of this pair of opposites.

There is Maithuna (Sexual Magic) within the White Tantra of India and Tibet.

Buddhist White Tantra, Chinese Taoism, and the legitimate Tibetan Yogas practice the Arcanum A.Z.F. Only the infrasexual pseudo-yogis and yoginis (that are so abundant in America and Asia) hate the Arcanum A.Z.F.

Chinese Alchemy is the foundation of the authentic schools of yoga. The yellow lodges are schools of regeneration. Infrasexual people mortally hate the schools of regeneration.

Schools of Regeneration

To regenerate oneself means to generate oneself anew, in other words, to recreate oneself, to create oneself anew. This matter about being born anew[108] is an absolutely sexual problem.

Neptune governs schools of regeneration; this planet has a cycle of 165 years. That cycle controls the periods of public and secret activities of these schools.

The esotericism of the schools of regeneration is the Arcanum A.Z.F. The masters of these schools teach their disciples the science that allows them to dissolve their ego. It is necessary that the Being — which is not the ego — be born within us. Something old must die within the human being and something new must be born within.

---

106 Chinese 阴阳, literally "bright-black."
107 Chinese 太極, "supreme pole (goal)," a term for the Absolute.
108 A reference to the Christian notion of being "born again."

Regeneration signifies the creation of a new cosmos within us. This type of creation is possible only by working with the lion of fire. Uranus controls the chakras of the sexual glands, yet the schools of regeneration are Neptunian.

Eminent astrologers affirm that Neptune influences the pineal gland; the potency of the pineal gland depends on the sexual potency.

Great schools of regeneration have existed throughout the course of history; it is enough for us to remember the Rosicrucian alchemical school that became secret in the year 1620. Likewise, it comes into our memory the schools of Aryavarta Ashrama of Tibet, as well as the sect of the Manicheans of Persian origin, and the famous Sufis with their sacred dances, the Templars, etc. All of these were schools of regeneration. The "coitus reservatus" is practiced in all of them. The schools of regeneration constitute the golden chain of the White Lodge.

Fire Projection

The Kundalini can be aimed or projected to any chakra or to any distant place. Within the cervical vertebrae, the Kundalini can take the shape of a quetzal (the bird of Minerva). In the supreme moment of the sacred copulation, we can send this fiery bird to each of the seven chakras in order to awaken them totally. The two quetzals (one from the man and one from the woman) are nourished with water (the ens seminis) of the well (sex).

QUETZAL

Man and woman can command the quetzal and the fiery bird will obey. The powerful mantra **Jao Ri** is the secret clue that grants us the power of commanding the quetzal. This miraculous bird can transform our face or make us invisible if we are in very grave danger, it can also awaken within us any chakra of the astral body or heal any distant ill person, etc.

Imagination

There are two types of imagination: mechanical imagination (fantasies) and cognizant imagination (clairvoyance). Gnostic students must learn how to use their cognizant imagination.

PRACTICE

1. The disciple must quiet the mind and emotions while seated in a comfortable chair or while lying down (face up, in a reclining position).
2. Now, imagine the marvelous quetzal floating above your head.
3. Mentally vocalize the mantra of power **Proweoa**. The quetzal's divine image (splendid bird of beautifully intense emerald feathers, golden green plume with a red belly and long green feathers yet with a white undertail) will come to your imagination with this mantra. The disciple must become familiar with this bird and learn how to handle it. You can awaken your internal powers with this fiery bird.
4. The mantra **Proweoa** (utilized often by the schools of the great chain) allow us to bring into our cognizant imagination any image from the superior worlds; this is how we can see clairvoyantly. The alchemist must utilize this mantra during the trance-state of Sexual Magic in order to see the quetzal.

Arcanum 12

We must now study the Twelfth Arcanum of the Tarot.

Chinese tradition mentions the ten stems (tiāngān 天 十) and the twelve branches. It is necessary to know that the seven chakras and the five senses are the twelve faculties. The universe emerged from the Chinese 混沌 Hun-tun; this is the primordial chaos. The ten stems and the twelve branches emerged from the chaos, which in Alchemy is the ens seminis, the lapis philosophorum or the Philosophical Stone.

The entire misterium magnum[109] is found enclosed within this sum matter.

The alchemist must extract the potable gold from this menstrum universale[110] in order to achieve the blending of the cross with the triangle. Before achieving this amalgamation, we do not have a true existence.

The four bodies of sin (physical, vital, astral, and mental) are controlled by the ego.

The ego, the "I," is not the Divine Being of the human being. Indeed, the "I" is the total sum of successive "I"s, for instance: John the drunkard, John the tenor, John the intellectual, John the religious, John the merchant, John the youth, John the mature one, John the elder, etc... all are a succession of "I"s, a succession of phantoms that inevitably are condemned to death. The "I" does not constitute the whole of what the human being is. John fought in the tavern, John is now religious, John is now a bandit; to that end, every person is a dance of Johns, so who is the true John? Therefore, if we do not escape from the fallacy of all of these multiple "I"s, we cannot assert that we have a true existence.

Present humans have not incarnated their immortal soul (their Divine Being) yet. Thus, from this point of view we can asseverate that present humans have no true existence yet. The annihilation of all of those false and mistakenly called centers of consciousness is only possible by denying oneself.

---

109 Latin, "great mystery."
110 Universal solvent, a substance used to dissolve another substance.

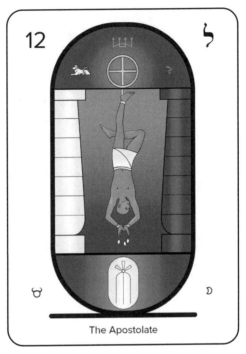

The Apostolate

ARCANUM 12

We are astonished when seeing how so many students of esotericism (as if they were great masters) attire themselves with tunics and bestow beautiful sounding names upon themselves, when indeed they do not even have true existence.

It is necessary to annihilate the "I" in order to attain true existence. Do you want to drink? Then do not drink; do you want to smoke? Then do not smoke. Did they strike your right cheek? Then present your left cheek to them.

The supreme negation of oneself is found in the coitus. Not to ejaculate the ens seminis in the supreme moment is an absolute sacrifice of the "I." The outcome of that negation of oneself is the awakening of the Kundalini.

The fire burns the evil scoria and in the end it absolutely dissolves the "I." The fire is the potable Gold.

The Great Work

The Twelfth Arcanum of the Tarot represents the Great Work. On this card, we see a man that hangs from one foot. The hands of this man are tied in such a way that they form an apex of an inverted triangle; with his legs, he forms a cross that is over the triangle (over the rest of his body). The objective of the entire work is to acquire the soul, in other words, to attain the amalgamation of the cross with the triangle. This is the Great Work. The Twelfth Card of the Tarot is Sexual Alchemy. The cross / man must join the triangle / spirit by means of the sexual fire.

According to the Chinese, the god 后稷 Hou Ji (the Adam-Christ) was born at midnight, on the fourth day of the tenth moon. Precisely at twelve years old, the virgin 姜嫄 Jiang Yuan, while walking along the shore of the river (the seminal liquid), conceived the Christ in her womb while placing her foot on the print of the Great Man.[111]

You must study these dates 4, 10, 12 under the light of the lectures 4, 10, and 12 of this present course.

White and Black Tantra

There are two types of Tantra in the East. The ejaculation of the ens seminis is not taught in positive Tantra, whereas the ejaculation of the ens seminis is practiced in Black Tantra. There is also Grey Tantra, however this type of Tantra is not concerned with whether or not seminal ejaculation occurs; this Tantra is very dangerous because it can easily mislead the students towards negative Tantra (Black Tantra).

Positive sexual yoga is practiced without the ejaculation of the seminal liquor. There is a Tantric sadhana[112] for the connection of the membrum virile and the genitalia murielis; the sexual connection is performed after an interchange of caresses between man and woman. The couple remains quiet, with their minds empty so that their "I" does not interfere, thus

---

111 上帝 Shangdi, "supreme deity."
112 Sanskrit, spiritual practice.

this is how they reach ecstasy[113] during the Tantric sadhana. The entire work is performed by the Tantric yogis under the guidance of a guru. The only significant thing (in Tantra) that comes from India is White Tantra, because it forbids the ejaculation of the ens seminis.

TWELFTH KEY OF BASIL VALENTINE

Twelfth Key of Basil Valentine

In the twelfth key of Basil Valentine, the Twelfth Arcanum is profoundly studied, thus it is important to comprehend it.

As the lion transforms the serpent into its own flesh when he devours it, likewise the Philosophical Stone or powder of projection (red lion and living fire) has the power to transmute or transform all imperfect metals into his own igneous substance. The vile metals are the false values that constitute the "I." The fire transmutes them, and then the "I" is dissolved. Thus, this is how we acquire soul, Being; this is to be different.

Without the fermentation of the Gold (fire), no one can arrange the Philosophical Stone or develop the tincturing virtue. The tincture of the fire has the power to penetrate all

---

113 This ecstasy is Samadhi, a state of consciousness, not physical sensations.

of the internal bodies in order to radically transform them. Similar is united to its similar in order to transform it. The fire transforms the lead of the personality into the gold of the spirit.

Three serpents that symbolize Mercury, Sulfur, and Salt represent the synthesis of the Great Work. The phoenix bird rises from within its own ashes. The alchemists must work for twelve hours in order to attain the fermentation of the gold. Behold here the Twelfth Arcanum of Kabbalah. Whosoever possesses the fermented gold can have the joy of truly being.

Non-identification

The present human is a dormant machine. If you want to awaken from the profound dream in which you live, then do not identify with pleasures, desires, emotions, dramas, scenes of your life, etc... Call yourself to vigilance in each step; remember good disciple, that people are dreaming. Observe people and their dreams, analyze all of those dreams in which humanity lives, but do not identify with those dreams so that you can awaken.

People believe they are awakened because they are not sleeping in their beds; regardless, they have their consciousness profoundly asleep, thus they dream. Everything that you see amongst the people is simply dreams. Nevertheless, remember that to not identify with one's dreams does not mean to abandon your duties as a father, a mother, a son or daughter, etc. However, do not identify; thus this is how you will awaken from the profound dream in which you live.

ARCANUM 13

Arcanum 13

Let us now study the Thirteenth Arcanum of the Tarot. This is the arcanum of death.

Indeed, death is the return into the womb. Life and death are two phenomena of the same thing. Death is the difference of whole numbers; only the values of the consciousness are what remain after this mathematical operation is completed. These values (when seen clairvoyantly) look like a legion of phantoms that continue. The return of these values occurs in the mechanism of Nature. Indeed, the soul does not reincarnate, because the human being does not have his soul incarnated yet. Only the values are what return and incarnate.

The Embryo of a Soul

Present humans only have an embryo of a soul; this embryo can be developed and strengthened by means of Sexual Magic. Often this embryo believes that it is whole and forgets its origin; when this occurs, we totally fail.

Immortality

Humans must attain immortality, because they do not have it. Only those who have incarnated their soul are immortal.

Mind

It is stated that humans have one mind, yet we state that each human has many minds. Each phantom from the pluralized "I" has its own mind and even self-independence. Present humans are dormant machines driven by the legion of "I's." We need to engender the Christ-Mind.

Christ-Astral

Whosoever engenders the Christ-Astral can become immortal within that body. The Christ-Astral is born only by Sexual

Magic. People who engendered the Christ-Astral in past incarnations retain the memory of their past lives, and with their Christ-Astral they know how to depart and return into their physical body at will. These people are immortal.

True Identity

Common, ordinary people do not have a true identity, because only those phantoms of the pluralized "I" are expressed through them. Thus, after death each human is a legion.

Soul

Whosoever incarnates their Soul acquires true identity and thus already IS. Present humans are not Self-realized beings.

Willpower

Present humans confuse the force of desire with willpower. We need to engender Christ-Will.

The Laboratorium Oratorium

The adept and his/her spouse must work together in the laboratorium oratorium. The king and the queen perform their alchemical combinations in the nuptial chamber [SEE FIGURE A]. Outside of this royal chamber, the ravens of putrefaction devour the Sun and the Moon (blackening and putrefaction of the internal chrysalides or bodies of sin).

Within a tomb of glass [FIGURE B] the bodies of sin become putrid; this tomb of glass is the glass of alchemy.

The souls rise up to fly [FIGURE C] (symbol of the butterfly that comes out from within the chrysalis, a symbol of the Christified vehicles that come out from within their chrysalides).

A hermaphrodite body (Sun and Moon) comes to life with the heavenly influence of the dew (the ens seminis). The hermaphrodite body [FIGURE D] encompasses the internal Christic

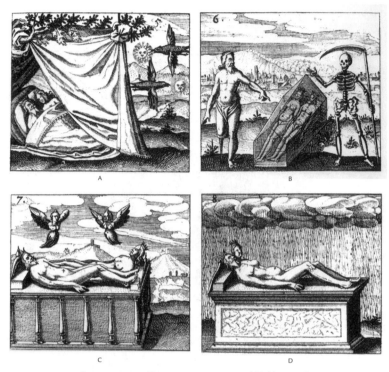

ENGRAVINGS FROM PHILOSOPHIA REFORMATA, BY J. D. MYLIUS, 1622

vehicles that were engendered by means of Sexual Magic. All of these Christic vehicles interpenetrate without confusion. When a person has these vehicles, he/she can incarnate his/her soul. Without having these Christic bodies, no "human being" is a true human being.

The Retort of Alchemy

The materia prima of the Great Work is within the alchemical retort. This venerable matter is very volatile and it is not still; its special characteristic is its instability and variability. This venerable matter boils and dissolves by lighting the sexual fire under the retort of Alchemy.

When arriving at this step of the work, the venerable matter has converted itself into a very gorgeous child glowing with

S. Trismosin, Splendor solis, 16th century

"Those who have succeeded in creating all of these
Christic vehicles within the alchemical retort can
incarnate their soul totally and integrally."

beauty. This is the Soma Psuchikon,[114] the body of gold; we can consciously visit all the departments of the kingdom with this precious vehicle. Then, by giving new properties to this alchemical alloy, the Christ-Astral appears within the astral phantom; this is a very precious child who grants us immortality. After this second body has been created, the problem of integrally comprehending all of the acquired powers and knowledge arises. This problem is only resolved when the Christic intelligence is given to this alchemical alloy. Thus, the precious vehicle of the Christ-Mind happily rises from within the retort of the laboratory; this vehicle emerges from within the mental phantom.

After this work has been completed, something is still missing. Christ-Will is what is missing. Thus by intensely reheating the retort of the laboratory, a divine child comes to life; this is the Christ-Will, the divine body of the Soul. Those who have succeeded in creating all of these Christic vehicles within the alchemical retort can incarnate their soul totally and integrally. Only those who achieve the incarnation of their soul deserve the precious title of human. Only these true humans can elevate themselves up to the kingdom of the human being, the superhuman. Only these true human beings can receive the Elixir of Long Life.

No human-sketch-creature can incarnate the soul; not a single soulless creature can receive the Elixir of Long Life. It is necessary to create the Christic vehicles in order to incarnate the soul. Only those who incarnate their soul have the right to receive the marvelous elixir that elevates us to the kingdom of the superhuman being.

Serpents' Scales, Butterflies' Chrysalides

After each one of the great Initiations of Major Mysteries, the ethereal, astral, mental, and causal phantoms are similar to scales that have been discarded by serpents, or as chrysali-

---

114 from Greek Soma Psyche eikon: Soma meaning "body"; ψυχικός Psuch (psyche) " soul ", and ikon derives from Eikōn meaning "image." Literally, "the Soul Body Image."

des that have been discarded by butterflies (after they have flown away). Precisely after the great initiations is a work for humans, angels, and gods: to disintegrate the shells and to dissolve the pluralized "I." Ahamkara,[115] the karmic remnants of the gods, are precisely those phantom-like "I's."

Elixir of Long Life

Every true human being that incarnates the soul can ask for the Elixir of Long Life. This is a gas of immaculate whiteness. That gas is deposited in the vital depths of the human organism.

Resurrection

On the third day after the death of his physical body, the initiate (in his astral body, accompanied by the divine hierarchies) goes to his holy sepulcher. The initiate then invokes his physical body (with the help of the divine hierarchies); thus his physical body gets up and penetrates hyperspace. This is how the initiate achieves the escape from the grave.

In the supersensible worlds of hyperspace, holy women treat the body of the initiate with perfumes and aromatic ointments. Then, by obeying superior orders, the physical body penetrates within the astral body (through the top of his sidereal head). This is how the master once again possesses his physical body. This is the gift of Cupid.

After the resurrection, the master does not die again; he is eternal.

The Yogi-Christ from India, the immortal Babaji, and his immortal sister Mataji, live with the same physical bodies they had more than a million years ago. These immortal beings are the watchers of the Guardian Wall that protects humanity.

The Great Service

Immortal beings can appear and disappear instantaneously. They can make themselves visible in the physical world.

---

115 Sanskrit "pride, egotism, conception of one's individuality, arrogance."

Cagliostro, St. Germain, Quetzalcoatl, and many other immortal masters have performed great works in the world.

The Superhuman

First, we must become complete humans; thereafter (after resurrection) we elevate ourselves into the kingdom of the superhuman. Present humans are nothing more than human phantoms.

Temperance

ARCANUM 14

Arcanum 14

Beloved disciples, let us now study the Fourteenth Arcanum of the Tarot. It is convenient to state that the profound wisdom of this arcanum is classically divided into three parts:

1. Transmutation
2. Transformation
3. Transubstantiation

Let us study each of these separately.

1. Transmutation

In the Fourteenth Arcanum, there is an angel with the sun on her forehead. If we observe the angel will see that she has the square and the triangle of Gnostic esotericism on her vesture. The angel has a cup in each hand and mixes the substances of the cups together. One cup has the white elixir and the other the red elixir. The Elixir of Long Life is the outcome of the intelligent mixture of these two substances.

When the septenary (7) man is sexually united with the septenary woman, the sum is the Fourteenth Arcanum of the Tarot. Moreover, it is important to state that both the man and the woman have seven principles, and that the most important and fastest center of the human being is the sexual center.

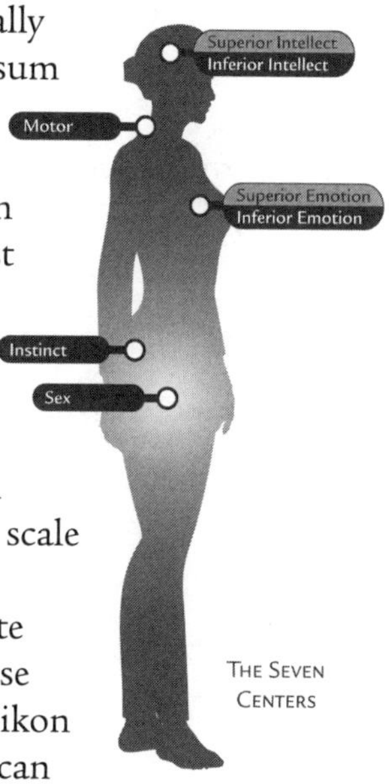

The process of creating a new being (the true human being) is performed with the laws of the musical octaves. The seven notes of the musical scale are the foundation of all creation. If we transmute the creative energy, we initiate a new octave in the ethereal world, whose outcome is the birth of To Soma Psuchikon (the wedding garment of the soul). We can

Superior Intellect
Inferior Intellect

Motor

Superior Emotion
Inferior Emotion

Instinct

Sex

THE SEVEN
CENTERS

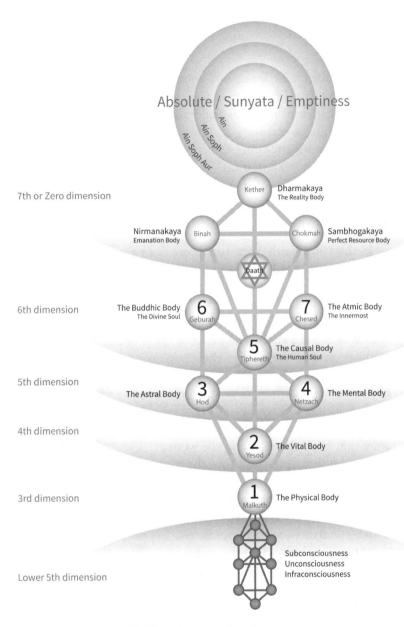

Absolute / Sunyata / Emptiness

Ain
Ain Soph
Ain Soph Aur

7th or Zero dimension

Kether — Dharmakaya
The Reality Body

Nirmanakaya — Binah   Chokmah — Sambhogakaya
Emanation Body   Perfect Resource Body

Daath

6th dimension

The Buddhic Body — **6** Geburah   **7** Chesed — The Atmic Body
The Divine Soul   The Innermost

5 Tiphereth — The Causal Body
The Human Soul

5th dimension

The Astral Body — **3** Hod   **4** Netzach — The Mental Body

4th dimension

2 Yesod — The Vital Body

3rd dimension

1 Malkuth — The Physical Body

Subconsciousness
Unconsciousness
Infraconsciousness

Lower 5th dimension

THE TREE OF LIFE AND THE SEVEN BODIES

consciously penetrate all of the departments of the kingdom with this vehicle.

A third octave will permit us to engender the true astral body, the Christ-Astral (the Christic astral body). When reaching these heights, the old astral, the phantom, is left reduced to an empty shell, which, little by little, will be disintegrated.

A fourth octave permits us to engender the Christ-Mind. This vehicle gives us true wisdom and unity of thought. Only the one who engenders the Christ-Mind has the right to say, "I have a mental body." The present mental body is only a phantom-like body. This phantom-like-shaped mind really converts itself into an empty shell when the true mind is born. Then, the old mental carcass is disintegrated and reduced to cosmic dust.

In the fifth musical octave, the true causal body is engendered. When reaching that height, we incarnate the soul, then we have a real existence. Before that moment, we do not have a real existence.

WORK WITH THE PROSTATIC/UTERINE CHAKRA

Immediately after finishing the daily work with the Arcanum A.Z.F., the alchemist should lie down in the dorsal decubitus position (facing up); he/she must work with his/her prostatic/uterine chakra. This is a very important chakra in high magic.

The alchemist must inhale the vital air, then retain the breath and in those moments direct the nervous currents towards the prostate/uterus with the intention of closing the sphincters between the seminal vessels and the urethra.

The effort of sending the electro-magnetic currents must be similar to the supreme effort that a woman does when giving birth. The woman moans in those moments—in other words, her larynx emits the moaning sound of the letter "M." Krumm-Heller stated that initiation must start with the letter "M" and "S." If we want to be born in the internal worlds, then we must also utter the sound of the letter "M" (as when one moans). It is about being born, and we must be born.

Thereafter we slowly exhale; we wait for the breath to naturally return to us, and we inhale, we mentally pump the creative energy and make it rise through the two canals Ida and Pingala to the chalice (the brain). We continue repeating the exercise.

IMAGINATION AND WILLPOWER

Imagination is feminine, and willpower is masculine. When we work with the prostatic/uterine chakra, we must unite these two powers in an alchemical wedding in order to promote the ascension of the creative energy. We do this first through the sympathetic cords of the physical body; second through the sympathetic cords of the ethereal body; third through the sympathetic cords of the body of desires; fourth through the sympathetic cords of the mental body; fifth through the sympathetic cords of the causal body. Advanced students must carry the creative energy even to the Ain Soph.

HEART

After a certain time of practice, students must learn how to direct their creative energy from their brain to their heart.

The Fourteenth Arcanum is the Arcanum of Temperance.

2. Transformation (Shapeshifting)

In the Jinn state, a body can shapeshift easily. Circe shapeshifted men into pigs. Legend states that Apuleius shapeshifted himself into an ass.

To manage shapeshifting, the following Latin mantras are used: "**Est Sit**, **Esto**, **Fiat**." Only while in a Jinn state can we adopt any type of shapeshifting.

CLUE FOR JINN STATE

The devotee must sit at a table and cross the arms, placing them on the table; while resting one's head on one's arms, one must willingly fall asleep. The student must relax the mind by emptying it from any type of thoughts until it is blank. Thereafter, imagine the slumber state (that precedes the dreaming state); identify with it and fall asleep. When the student feels that one is slumbering, one should get up from the chair (but keep the slumber state as if one was a somnambulist) and attempt a long jump, as far as possible, with the intention of submerging oneself within hyperspace (with the physical body). Thereafter with a pencil, one must mark the exact spot on the floor where one's foot landed.

As the student practices this exercise, one will notice that each time the length of the jump is longer and longer. Finally, the day will arrive in which one will perform a jump that is beyond average. This will give the student joy because it will indicate that the physical body is now entering into hyperspace. Finally, constancy, patience, willpower and tenacity will grant triumph to the student; thus, on any given day the student will definitively sustain the physical body in hyperspace. With the physical body one will penetrate into the internal worlds; one will be in "Jinn state." Then within a few moments, one will be able to transport oneself to any place on earth. One will become an investigator of the superior worlds.

GENII OF JINN SCIENCE

Before initiating the former Jinn practice, the student must invoke the genii of Jinn science. The devotee will invoke the Master Oguara many times, as follows:

> "I believe in God, I believe in Oguara and in all the genii of the Jinn Science, take me with my physical body to all the temples of Jinn Science. Oguara! Oguara! Oguara! Carry me."

This invocation must be repeated thousands of times before falling asleep.

3. Transubstantiation

The Last Supper of the beloved savior of the world comes from archaic epochs. The great Lord of Atlantis also practiced this ceremony as Jesus Christ did.

THE LAST SUPPER

This is a blood ceremony, a blood pact. Each of the apostles put their blood into a cup and then they mixed their blood with the royal blood of the Beloved One within the chalice of the Last Supper (the Holy Grail). Thus, this is how the astral bodies of the apostles joined the astral body of Christ, by means of this blood pact. The apostles drank the blood contained within the chalice, and Jesus likewise drank from it.

The Holy Gnostic Unction is united to the Last Supper through this blood pact. When the Christic atoms (solar astral atoms) descend into the bread and the wine, they are in fact converted into the flesh and blood of the cosmic Christ. This is the mystery of the transubstantiation.

Arcanum 15

Let us now study the Fifteenth Arcanum of the Tarot. We are going to study the male goat of Mendes, Typhon Baphomet, the devil. The alchemist must steal the fire from the devil. When we work with the Arcanum A.Z.F., we steal the fire from the devil; this is how we transform ourselves into gods.

The esoteric pentagram shines upon the forehead of the male goat. The Caduceus of Mercury replaces the sexual organs. In synthesis, we can state that the Caduceus of Mercury represents the sexual organs. Every alchemist needs to work with the Caduceus of Mercury. This work is performed by means of transmutation. The star of five points shines when we steal the fire from the devil.

We need to develop the Kundalini and to dissolve the "I," only in this way can we attain liberation.

The Work with the Demon

The initiates of the fourth path, which is "The Path of the Astute Man," choose "to work with the devil" on the process of the dissolution of their "I." The tenebrous ones violently attack anyone who works in the dissolution of their "I." This is why even though the intiates are not demons, they are nonetheless used to being surrounded by demons. When non-initiated seers clairvoy-antly see a human being like this, they mistakenly misjudge

BAPHOMET

Passion

ARCANUM 15

him and end up calumniating him when qualifying him as a
demon.

The initiates of "The Path of the Astute Man" are enig-
matic. Disciples from the path become confused when they
contemplate black candles upon the altars of these initiates;
then, as usual, they mistakenly misjudge them.

Techniques for the Dissolution of the Ego

The "I" exerts control over the five inferior centers of the
human machine. These five centers are the intellectual, emotional, motor (movement), instinctual, and sexual.[116]

The "I" cannot control the two superior centers of the
human being, which are the superior intellect and superior
emotion.

If we want to dissolve the "I," we must study it in the inferior centers. We need comprehension.[117] It is urgent to comprehend the actions and reactions of each of the five inferior
centers of the human machine.

The "I" exerts control over these inferior centers, therefore
we walk on the path of the dissolution of the "I" by in depth
comprehension of the activity of each of the five inferior
centers.

Intellect and Emotion

Two people react differently before any given representation;
what is pleasant for one person could be unpleasant for the
other. The difference lies in the fact that one person perceives
and judges the representation through the intellect, while the
other does it through emotions (the representation touches
the feelings). Therefore, we must learn how to differentiate
intellect from emotion.

One thing is the intellect, and another is emotion. Within
the intellect there is an entire play of actions and reactions
that must be carefully comprehended. Within our emotions
there are affections that must be crucified, emotions that must

116 See illustration on page 103.
117 See glossary.

be studied, and in general an entire mechanism of actions and reactions that can easily be misplaced and confounded with the activities of the intellect.

Movement

We need to self-discover ourselves and comprehend our habits in depth. We must not allow our life to continue to develop mechanically.

It seems incredible that we live within the molds of habits, and that we do not know the molds that condition our life. We need to study our habits. We need to comprehend our habits. We need to self-observe the way we speak, the way we dress, the way we walk, etc.

Habits belong to the center of movement. Football, tennis and all sports in general belong to this center. When the intellect interferes in the center of movement, it destroys and damages it, because the intellect is too slow and the center of movement is very fast. When a typist works, he works with the center of movement; he can commit a mistake in his typing if his intellect interferes with his movements. A man driving a car could suffer an accident if his intellect interferes with his movements.

Instinct

There are various types of instincts: the instinct of preservation, the sexual instinct, etc. There are also many perversions of instinct.

Deep within every human being there are sub-human, instinctual forces that paralyze the true spirit of love and charity. These demonic forces must first be comprehended, then brought under control and eliminated. These bestial forces are: criminal instincts, lust, cowardliness, fear, etc. We must comprehend and subdue these bestial forces before we can dissolve them.

Sex

Sex is the fifth power of the human being. Sex can liberate or enslave the human being. No one can attain integrity, no one can be deeply Self-realized, without sexual energy.

Sex is the power of the soul. The integral human being is achieved with the absolute fusion of the masculine and feminine poles of the soul. Sexual force develops, evolves and progresses on seven levels (the seven levels of the soul).

In the physical world, sex is a blind force of mutual attraction. In the astral world, sexual attraction is based on the affinity of types according to their polarities and essences. In the mental plane, sexual attraction occurs according to the laws of mental polarity and affinity. In the causal plane, sexual attraction takes place on the basis of conscious will. It is precisely on this plane of natural causes where the complete union of the soul is consciously performed. Indeed, no one can attain the complete glory of the perfect matrimony without having attained this fourth state of human integration.

We need to comprehend in depth the entire sexual problem. We must transcend the mechanicity of sex.

We need to know how to procreate children of wisdom. In the supreme moment of conception, human essences are completely open to all types of influences. Thus, the state of purity of the parents and their willpower used in order not to spill the cup of Hermes is all that can protect us against the terrible danger that the spermatozoon and the ovum face regarding the infiltration of subhuman substances of the bestial egos that want to reincorporate.

ADULTERY

Since a woman's body is a passive and receptive element, it is clear that her body collects and stores more of the results of the sexual acts than all of those men who commit adultery with her; those results are atomic substances from the men with whom she has had sexual intercourse. Therefore, when someone has sexual intercourse with a person who has been with another partner or other partners, both then absorb the atomic essences of the other partners and poison themselves with them. This is a very grave problem for those brothers and sisters who are dissolving the "I" because then, not only do they have to fight against their own errors and defects, but more over, they have to fight against the errors and defects of those other partners with whom they had sexual intercourse.

Death of Satan

We discover the entire process of the "I" by comprehending the inner activities of each one of the five inferior centers. The outcome of this self-discovery is the absolute death of Baphomet or Satan (the tenebrous lunar "I" or sinning Adam).

We Need to Be Integral

Integration has seven perfectly defined steps:

First: Mineral state, dominion of the physical body and its five centers.

Second: Vegetal state, absolute control over the astral body and of its chakras, discs or magnetic wheels. This vehicle represents the vegetal state.

Third: Humanization of the mental body. Ordinarily, the phantasmal mental body of every human being has an animal face and an animal figure; it is animalized. When the mental matter is transformed into the Christ-Mind, we achieve mental humanization. The mind represents the intellectual animal; presently we are human only in our physical appearance, because in our depths we are still animals. In the mental plane each one has the animal figure that corresponds to his individual character.

Fourth: The sexual function is the basic foundation of the Human Soul. Those who transmute their sexual energies have the right to incarnate their soul.

Fifth: The fifth degree of integration is represented in
           any perfect human being.

Sixth: Universal, infinite compassion.

Seventh: This seventh definitive step is only possible within
           human-gods. These are superhumans.

The Mystery of Baphomet

It is indeed true and certain that the mystery of Baphomet
is sexual alchemy. We transform the lead of our personality
into the gold of the spirit based on rigorous comprehension
and sexual transmutation. This is how the "I" is annihilated.

The rose elaborates its perfume with the mud of the earth;
the perfume of the rose is transmuted mud.

The Door of Eden

Sex is the door of Eden. The guardian of this door is the
Assyrian sphinx, the Egyptian sphinx, the bull (golden calf) of
Moses with the sword between its paws. This is the psychological "I" reflected in the Baphomet that with his sword drives
out from the threshold all of those who are not prepared. The
enemy is within us; we need to work with the demon in order
to dissolve it. We need to steal the fire from the devil.

Fragility

ARCANUM 16

Arcanum 16

Let us study now the Sixteenth Arcanum of the Tarot. This is the arcanum of the Fulminated Tower. This is the Tower of Babel.[118]

Two personages are precipitated to the bottom of the abyss. One of these personages when falling with his head downwards and his legs and arms outstretched represent the inverted pentagram. Many are the initiates that allow themselves to fall; many are the fulminated towers. Any initiate that spills the cup of Hermes falls inevitably. The legend of the fallen angels has been repeated and will be repeated eternally.

Presently many fallen gods live in the world. They are now camouflaged in the bodies of human beings.

Human Specter

Present humans are soulless creatures. When death arrives for them, only the human specter continues!

The embryo of the soul escapes from within this specter.

The post-mortem states mentioned by esotericists correspond to the embryo of the soul. This embryo returns to its true Being who normally lives in the causal world.

An in-depth analysis takes us to the conclusion that the human specter is a den of filthy demons. The conclusion is that after death, the present humans are transformed into a legion of demons that continue on. Indeed, the physical human person dies, because present humans are not immortal. Nonetheless, present humans believe themselves to be immortal and powerful, but their breaking point of arrogance is fulminated by the ray of death, and from their Tower of Babel they roll into the abyss. This is fatality.

Christ-Astral and Christ-Mind

Present humans have two centers that they do not use: superior intellect and superior emotion. These are two divine centers, the true instruments of the eternal and imperishable humans with soul. We can profoundly study the great mysteries of life and death with these two superior centers. It has been said to us that with these two superior centers we can even penetrate into the Great Reality that is far beyond time and eternity.

Those who believe that they already use these two centers without having engendered the vehicle of the Christ-Mind and the vehicle of the Christ-Astral are completely mistaken, because is necessary to engender these two vehicles in order to clothe the superior intellect and the superior emotion (only by means of the Arcanum A.Z.F. is it possible to engender these two superior vehicles). The Christ-Astral is born in the third Initiation of Major Mysteries, and the Christ-Mind is born in the fourth Initiation of Major Mysteries. Therefore, the astral and mental bodies studied by esotericists and often referred to by Theosophy are just miserable specters of death that eventually will be fulminated by the terrible ray of cosmic justice. Thus, this is how the Tower of Babel along with Satan will roll into the abyss.

Immortality

Whosoever possesses the astral and mental bodies becomes absolutely immortal. When we study these Christic vehicles and compare them with the astral and mental vehicles that are used by the defunct, then we find the following differences:

The Christ-Astral shines marvelously, whereas the astral of death does not shine because it is just a fatal shadow.

The Christ-Mind shines gloriously, whereas the mind of death does not shine.

The Christ-Astral is clean from passions, whereas the astral of death is a vehicle for animal passions.

The Christ-Mind has an angelical, divine figure, whereas the mind of death has an animal figure.

The Christ-Astral has the Kundalini and the chakras awakened, whereas the astral of death does not have the Kundalini awakened and if by chance it has the chakras awakened (by means of any genre of esoteric discipline) they shine like fatuous fires within the darkness of the abyss.

Conclusion: the Christ-human is immortal, whereas the terrestrial human is not. The Christ-human shines like the Sun, whereas the terrestrial human is just a shadow. The Christ-human is a Self-realized Being!

What is Fundamental

Those students of esotericism that practice esoteric exercises without working with the Arcanum A.Z.F. are similar to the man that builds his house upon the sands; his building will roll into the abyss.[119] We must build upon the living rock: this rock is sex. Whosoever develops his chakras within the specter of death will roll into the abyss; his temple will be a fulminated tower.

Whosoever engenders their Christic bodies with the Arcanum A.Z.F. and works with the development of their chakras become living Christs.

The Awakening of the Consciousness

It is necessary to awaken the consciousness in order not to fall into the abyss of perdition. Presently, there are many leaders of esoteric groups who have their consciousness profoundly asleep, blind leaders guiding the blind. All of them will roll into the abyss. This is the law.

Present human beings live absolutely asleep; for example, if suddenly during a football game a group of football players

---

119 "Therefore whosoever heareth these sayings of mine, and doeth them, I will liken him unto a wise man, which built his house upon a rock: And the rain descended, and the floods came, and the winds blew, and beat upon that house; and it fell not: for it was founded upon a rock. And every one that heareth these sayings of mine, and doeth them not, shall be likened unto a foolish man, which built his house upon the sand: And the rain descended, and the floods came, and the winds blew, and beat upon that house; and it fell: and great was the fall of it." —Matthew 7

were to awaken their consciousness, you can be absolutely sure that the game would unexpectedly end because all the players, ashamed of themselves, would immediately flee from the football field.

The fundamental cause of the profound dream in which the consciousness of humanity lives in is that which is called F-A-S-C-I-N-A-T-I-O-N. Football players' consciousnesses are profoundly fascinated by the game, thus they play sleepily. They appear to be playing while awake, but nonetheless the reality is that they are playing while asleep.

Ordinary Sleep

During the hours of rest (while the body ordinarily sleeps in bed), the ego travels out of the physical body many times to very remote places. However, out of the physical body, the ego is asleep; indeed, the ego takes its dreams into the supersensible worlds. In the internal worlds, carpenters are in their carpentry shops dreaming about all of the things they do in the physical world. Likewise, the blacksmiths are in their forges, the policemen are patrolling the streets, the tailors are in their tailor shops, the drunkards are in the bars, etc. All of them dream, all of them carry their dreams into their supersensible worlds. After death they continue repeating the same thing; their ego continues with the same dreams. Indeed, as in ordinary sleep the ego carries out their dreams, it is likewise after physical death.

Technique for the Awakening of the Consciousness

The technique for the awakening of the consciousness is based on Self-remembering. Every humanoid is found fascinated by many things, as we have already stated in the former paragraph. We forget ourselves when fascinated before a certain representation; we then dream.

During a public assembly people have launched themselves into violence. Gentlemen (when in their sane judgment) who are not capable of uttering a bad word, suddenly, while confounded by the multitudes, end up insulting and stoning their neighbor; behold here the power of fascination. One forgets oneself, then dreams and while dreaming one performs many completely absurd things. Shame and problems come after the dream has passed. Thus, it is necessary that the Gnostic student does not become fascinated with anything.

Gnostic students must remember themselves while in the presence of any interesting representation; they need to ask themselves the following questions, "Where am I? What am I doing here? Am I out of my physical body?"

Then, carefully observe everything that surrounds you. With inquisitive eyes look very carefully at the sky and all of the details of the internal worlds, at the strange colors, at the rare animal, at the beloved shadow of a deceased relative, etc. These details will confirm that you are out of your physical body Thus, this is how you will awaken your consciousness.

In those moments of reflection and self-remembrance, it is very useful to perform a small jump with the intention of floating in the surrounding environment. Thus, logically, if we float it is because we are out of our physical body.

If all those who dream would ask such reflective questions during their dream, then logically, they would awaken their consciousness. If after the death of the physical body, the ego would ask itself such reflective questions while in the presence of any representation, then it would instantaneously awaken. Unfortunately, such reflective questions are never uttered by the ego because during life it does not have the habit of doing so. Therefore, it is necessary to develop this habit and to intensely live it. Thus, only in this way is it possible to have the idea of asking ourselves such reflective questions during ordinary sleep and after death.

Therefore, the outcome of this practice is the awakening of our consciousness. Whosoever awakens their consciousness becomes clairvoyant. Whosoever awakens their consciousness lives completely awakened in the superior worlds during the sleep of the physical body.

The great masters do not dream; they are cognizant citizens of the supersensible worlds. The great masters work consciously and positively within the superior worlds during the sleep of their physical bodies. Therefore, it is necessary to awaken the consciousness in order not to go there blind. The blind can fall into the abyss.

The Arcanum Sixteen is very dangerous.

Memory

All memory is found deposited within the subconsciousness. Many initiates work in the internal worlds during ordinary sleep with cognizance; unfortunately, in the physical world they ignore this because they do not have good memory; thus we must learn how to handle the subconsciousness.

In the moments of physically awakening from ordinary sleep, we must command the subconsciousness as follows: "Subconsciousness, inform me of everything that I saw and heard while out of my physical body." Thereafter, practice a retrospective exercise in order to remember everything that you did while out of your physical body. Force your subconsciousness to work; give imperative orders to it in order to oblige it to inform you. Practice this exercise during the slumber state in those moments when you are awakening from your ordinary sleep.

Hope

ARCANUM 17

Arcanum 17

Seventeenth Arcanum of the Tarot: the hieroglyphic of this arcanum is a radiant star and eternal youth.

A naked woman appears in this arcanum. Over the earth she is pouring the sap of universal life from two jars, one made of gold and the other made of silver. If we carefully study the esoteric context of this arcanum, we then discover perfect alchemy. We need to work with the gold and with the silver, with the sun and with the moon so that we can incarnate the star. This star has eight points. Indeed, the star of eight points is Venus. Whosoever attains the Venustic Initiation has the joy of incarnating the dragon of wisdom (the inner Christ).

The seventeenth Arcanum is Hope.

The Gnostic student must be very careful with the work of the laboratorium oratorium. Since the betrayal of the sanctuary of Vulcan, the doctrine of Ahriman[120] was spread to many places; this is the doctrine of the Nicolaitans[121] that transform human beings into disgusting sub-lunar demons.

The left-hand[122] adepts paint their doctrine a very beautiful hue filled with ineffable and sublime mysticism. Many are the brothers and sisters of the path that have entered this tenebrous path. The basic foundation of the doctrine of the Nicholaitans consists of spilling the cup of Hermes. These offspring of darkness ejaculate the ens seminis during their practices of Sexual Magic. Billions of solar atoms are lost with the ejaculation of the ens seminis, which are replaced by billions of atoms from the secret enemy.

After the ejaculation, the creative organs collect these satanic atoms from the atomic infernos of the human being. When such satanic atoms intend to rise through the sympathetic canals to the brain, they are downwardly precipitated by the three rays: Father, Son, and Holy Spirit. When these types of tenebrous atoms descend, they violently crash against a master atom of the black lodge that resides in the fundamental chakra of the coccygeal bone. This atomic evil entity then receives a formidable impulse which gives it power to negatively awaken the fiery serpent of our magical powers (the Kundabuffer). In such a case, the fiery serpent descends downward to the atomic infernos of the human being and becomes the Kundabuffer (the tail of Satan). This is how the human being is definitively born in the abyss as a submerged sub-lunar type of demon. Many are the students of the luminous path that have gone astray by this dark path. It is good to remember that the great masters of the sanctuary of Vulcan fell under this subtle temptation and were converted into terrible, perverse demons.

The Narrow Door

There are many students of esotericism who are convinced that there are many paths to reach God. There are some who

---

120 Zoroastrian symbol of the adversary, Satan.
121 Christian Bible, Revelation 2:6,15
122 See glossary.

affirm that there are three paths; there are others who state that there are seven paths, and some others who believe that there are twelve paths. We state that the three, the seven and the twelve are reduced to one, which is sex. We have carefully studied the four gospels and have not found within any of the four gospels such an affirmation, which states that there are many ways in order to reach God. Conclusion, such an affirmation is absolutely false; indeed such an affirmation is a sophism in order to cheat those who are naïve.

Jesus, the chief of the souls, only spoke about one gate and about one strait and difficult narrow path. He never stated that there were many ways to reach God. The great Master Jesus textually stated the following:

> *"Strive to enter in at the strait gate: for many, I say unto you, will seek to enter in, and shall not be able. When once the master of the house is risen up, and hath shut to the door, and ye begin to stand without, and to knock at the door, saying, Lord, Lord, open unto us; and he shall answer and say unto you, I know you not whence ye are: Then shall ye begin to say, We have eaten and drunk in thy presence, and thou hast taught in our streets. But he shall say, I tell you, I know you not whence ye are; depart from me, all ye workers of iniquity. There shall be weeping and gnashing of teeth, when ye shall see Abraham, and Isaac, and Jacob, and all the prophets, in the kingdom of God, and you yourselves thrust out."* —Luke 13:24-28

Therefore, anyone who states the contrary is a flat-out liar.

Indeed, those who are saved are very few, because few are those who enter through that strait, narrow and difficult door of sex. Another door does not exist, it has never existed, and will never exist!

The mechanical evolution of Nature does not save anybody. Time does not save anybody. It is necessary to be born again, and this subject matter about birth has been, is, and will always be an absolutely sexual matter. Thus, anyone who wants to be born again has to work with the sap of life that is contained within the two sacred cups that the naked woman of the Seventeenth Arcanum has in her two hands.

The Three Rays

It has been stated unto us that there are three rays of the realization of the Inner Self. These three rays illuminate only one door and only one path: this is sex. The three rays are: the mystic, the yogic, and the perfect matrimony. Nevertheless, one does not advance a single step on the path of the razor's edge (spinal medulla) without the Arcanum A.Z.F.

Yoga

Yoga has been taught very badly in the Western World. Multitudes of pseudo-sapient yogis have spread the false belief that the true yogi must be an infrasexual (an enemy of sex). Some of these false yogis have never even visited India; they are infrasexual pseudo-yogis. These ignoramuses believe that they are going to achieve in-depth realization only with the yogic exercises, such as asanas, pranayamas, etc. Not only do they have such false beliefs, but what is worse is that they propagate them; thus, they misguide many people away from the difficult, straight, and narrow door that leads unto the light.

No authentically initiated yogi from India would ever think that he could achieve the realization of his inner Self with pranayamas or asanas, etc. Any legitimate yogi from India knows very well that such yogic exercises are only aids that are very useful for their health and for the development of their powers, etc. Only Westerners and pseudo-yogis have within their minds the belief that they can achieve realization of the Self with such exercises.

Sexual Magic is practiced very secretly within the ashrams of India. Any true yogi initiate from India works with the Arcanum A.Z.F. This is taught by the great yogis from India that have visited the Western world, and if it has not been taught by these great, initiated Hindustani yogis, if it has not been published in their books of yoga, it was in order to avoid scandals. You can be absolutely sure that the yogis who do not practice Sexual Magic will never achieve birth in the superior worlds. Thus, whosoever affirms the contrary is a liar, an impostor.

Astrology

In each lifetime, the human being is born under a different star. A wise man stated: "I raise my eyes towards the stars that will come to my rescue; nevertheless, I always guide myself with my star, which I carry within my inner Self." Indeed, that a star is always the same; it never changes in any of our lives; this is the Father Star. Thus, what is important for us is to incarnate the Father Star. Behold here the mystery of the Seventeenth Arcanum. When the sap that is contained within the cups of gold and silver is wisely combined and transmuted, it allows us to attain the incarnation of the star. Christ is the star, crucified on the cross.

Twilight

ARCANUM 18

Arcanum 18

Now, let us study the Eighteenth Arcanum of Kabbalah. This is the arcanum of Twilight. It is necessary for our Gnostic disciples to profoundly reflect on the esoteric context of this arcanum.

We have been strongly criticized for not continuing with the already known Hebraic monotony. Indeed, we do not want to follow the same Hebraic monotony. We, Gnostics, are only interested in that which is called C-O-M-P-R-E-H-E-N-S-I-O-N.

We want our students to comprehend each arcanum and thereafter develop it within themselves. First, we want our disciples to discover each arcanum within themselves, then subsequently within all of Nature.

The Eighteenth Arcanum is light and darkness, white magic and black magic. On the eighteenth card a dog and a wolf appear, howling at the moon. Two pyramids are found, one black and the other white, as well as the symbol of the scorpion at the bottom.

The number nine is found twice in the Eighteenth Arcanum: 9 + 9 = 18. Thus, the Ninth Sphere is repeated twice in this arcanum. We already know that the number one is positive and that the number two is negative. Therefore, if we repeat the ninth sphere twice, we then have sex in its two aspects: the first being the positive aspect and the second the negative aspect.

Now our disciples will comprehend why the Eighteenth Arcanum is light and darkness, white magic and black magic. The secret enemies of initiation are found in the Eighteenth Arcanum.

Beloved disciples, you must know that the Kundalini rises very slowly through the medullar canal. The ascension of the Kundalini, vertebra by vertebra, is performed very slowly according to the merits of the heart. Each vertebra represents certain virtues. The ascension to a certain vertebra is never acquired without having achieved the conditions of sanctity that are required for such a vertebra, which we long for.

Therefore, those who believe that once the Kundalini is awakened, it instantaneously rises to the head in order to leave us totally illuminated, are indeed learned ignoramuses.

In the Eighteenth Arcanum, we have to endure bloody battles against the tenebrous ones.

> *"Now the kingdom of heaven suffers violence and the violent take it by force."* –Matthew 11:12

Within the internal worlds, the tenebrous ones of the Eighteenth Arcanum violently assault the student. The devotee must endure terrible battles against these tenebrous ones.

The conquest of each vertebra in the dorsal spine signifies fights to the death against the shadow's adepts. Fortunately, those who work with the Kundalini receive the flaming sword and they defend themselves with it. Sometimes the student, too weary, yet still holding the sword in his hands, achieves the entrance into the temple.

Terrible are the efforts that the tenebrous ones exert in order to withdraw the student from the path of the razor's edge.

This path is full of dangers from within and from without. Many are those who begin, yet few are those who finish. The great majority deviate towards the black path.

Very subtle dangers that the student ignores are within the Eighteenth Arcanum.

The tenebrous gather in their temples in order to count the number of vertebrae conquered by the student. They represent each vertebra with a cup; thus upon the altar they place the same number of cups as the number of vertebrae conquered by the student. Thus, it is on this basis that they judge the neophyte and consider him a thief. The tenebrous ones' thoughts could be formulated as follows: "You have stolen these cups from us. You are stealing powers from us. You are a thief." The tenebrous never believe themselves to be evil, on the contrary they believe themselves to be wells of sanctity. Therefore, when they attack the student they do it with good intentions because they believe the student to be a thief of powers and that is all. Indeed, the abyss is filled with sincere but mistaken people; these are people with very good intentions.

The number nine is positive and negative at the same time. Now we can explain the mystery of the Eighteenth Arcanum.

In this disturbing arcanum we find all the potions and witchcraft of Thessaly. Here is the cuisine of Conidia; we can read (in the times of Horaccio) how this horrible witch of Rome made all of her potions. The books of the grimoires are full of tenebrous recipes which are obviously related to the Eighteenth Arcanum, such as erotic magical ceremonies, rites in order to be loved, dangerous potions, etc... All of this is the Eighteenth Arcanum.

We must warn the Gnostic students that the most dangerous potion that the tenebrous ones use in order to take the student off of the path of the razor's edge is the intellect.

Bluntly we warn our disciples that out of the billions of people who live in the world, only a small handful of souls (which we could count on our fingers) will be worth the angelic state! The rest, the great majority, is a lost harvest that will sink into the abyss forever.

To become an angel is very difficult. Neither time nor the mechanical evolution of Nature can ever convert the present human being into an angel, because this is a sexual subject matter.

Adam-Christ

In order for the Christ to be born within us, it is first necessary for the Buddha to be born in us.[123] When a person has engendered all of his internal vehicles, he then incarnates his Buddha and becomes a Buddha. We warn our students that the soul is not Christ.

There are many Buddhas in Asia that still do not have the Christ incarnated. Remember beloved disciples, that the resplendent dragon of wisdom is beyond any Buddha. The resplendent dragon of wisdom is the inner Christ of every human being that comes into the world.

---

123 Our inner Buddha is born in us with the fourth initiation of Major Mysteries. Christ can be incarnated after the fifth.

When the resplendent dragon of wisdom enters into the soul, then he is transformed into the soul and the soul is transformed into him. That which is called the Adam-Christ, the Son of Man, is the outcome of this divine and human mixture.

Cosmic Christ

It is necessary for our Gnostic disciples to comprehend that the resplendent dragon of wisdom (the inner Christ) of every human being that comes into the world, has no individuality. The latter is the outcome of the "I," and the Christ is not any type of "I." Thus, it is absurd to talk about the "I" Christ, when indeed the internal Christ does not have any type of "I."

The resplendent dragon of wisdom transcends beyond any type of "I" and beyond any individuality. The Beloved One is absolutely infinite and impersonal.

Solar Internal Bodies

Indeed, present humans still do not possess their internal vehicles. Present astral, mental, and causal vehicles that are used by humans are nothing more than mental formations that we need to disintegrate. Those mental formations constitute the human specter within which the "I" lives.

We need to engender the solar internal vehicles in order to incarnate the Buddha, and thereafter, the Christ. This is an absolutely sexual subject matter.

Renowned Incarnations

Living Buddhas are renowned incarnations. These are the unique cases in which the universal Spirit of Life incarnates and reincarnates. Within the rest of the ordinary people, only their values reincorporate, in other words, their "I", their ego, Satan. Indeed, Satan (the ego) only reincorporates in order to satisfy its desires, and that is all. The only reincarnations worthy of admiration are the living reincarnations. The Ninth Sphere in its positive aspect brings living Buddhas into the world, yet in its negative aspect it only brings memories (egos), specters of personalities that were physically alive and died. This is the fatal wheel. Now, you will comprehend the whole drama of the Eighteenth Arcanum. Positive nine plus negative nine is equal to eighteen.

The Embryo of the Soul

The embryo of soul lives within the specter and reincorporates together with the specter and with the "I." It is necessary to comprehend that the "I" and the embryo of the soul exist within any specter.

We have spoken about this in former lectures, yet it seems that many students have not yet understood this. Thus we clarify that the embryo of the soul, which every human has within, is not the Christ, because the Christ is not incarnated within present human beings yet. Only those who reach the Venustic Initiation incarnate the Christ and no one can reach said initiation without previously having incarnated one's Buddha of perfections.

Inspiration

ARCANUM 19

Arcanum 19

Let us now study the hieroglyphic of the Nineteenth Arcanum of the Tarot: a radiant sun and two children holding hands.

In the Egyptian Tarot, the hieroglyphic is of a man and a woman holding with their hands the symbolic Egyptian tau cross. This type of cross is phallic.

The Nineteenth Arcanum is the arcanum of the Alliance.

In the third lecture of our course, we broadly spoke about the Salt, the Sulfur, and the Mercury. Indeed, these are the passive instruments of the Great Work. The positive principle is the interior magnes[124] of Paracelsus.[125]

We need to transmute and thereafter sublimate the sexual energy to the heart. It is impossible to advance in the Great Work without the force of love. The psychological "I" does not know how to love, because the psychological "I" is desire.

It is easy to mistake desire with that which is called love. Desire is a substance that decomposes into thoughts, volitions, sentiments, romances, poetries, tenderness, sweetness, anger, hatred, violence, etc. The poison of desire always cheats people. Those who are in love always swear that they are loving, when in reality they are desiring.

Present humans do not know that which is called love. Nevertheless, we have within the most recondite parts of our Being a principle that loves. Unfortunately, we do not have this principle incarnated. This principle is the soul (the inner magnes of Paracelsus). If people had that soul-principle incarnated, then they could love. It is only possible to love from heart to heart, from soul to soul. Unfortunately, people only have Satan incarnated, and Satan does not know what love is. Satan only knows about desire, that is all.

Daily we see multitudes of lovers swearing eternal love to each other, yet after they satisfy their desire (that desire that they believed to be love) disillusionment arrives, along with

---

124 (Latin) Canon, principle or prima materia.
125 Renaissance physician, alchemist and philosopher.

disenchantment and total disappointment. Desire is a great swindler.

Whosoever wants to work in the Great Work has to annihilate desire. It is necessary to know how to love.

Love has its peculiar happiness and its infinite beauty.

People do not know that which is called love. Love is similar to the sentiments shown by a newborn baby. Love forgives everything, gives everything, it does not demand anything, it does not ask for anything, it only wants the best for the one it loves, and that is all. The true sentiment of love is perfect, and Satan knows nothing of perfection, because Satan is desire.

If you want to love, be prudent. Do not confuse love with desire. Do not allow yourself to be cheated by desire, the great swindler.

You have an embryo of a soul within, and this can love. Indeed, this is an embryonic love because it is an embryo of Soul. Yet, if you annihilate desire you will feel that spark of love. When you learn how to feel that spark, then that spark will become a flame, and you will experience that which is called love. Therefore, strengthen your embryo of soul with the blessed flame of love, and then you will achieve the miracle of your incarnation. It is necessary for you to be integral and that is only possible by loving.

In the Nineteenth Arcanum, a great alliance is established between two souls. Man and woman must kill desire in order to achieve the great alliance. If you want to incarnate your soul, you must then celebrate the great alliance of the Nineteenth Arcanum.

Reflect a little; until now you are just a living specter, a sleeping specter. You, wretched specter, sleep during the slumber of your physical body, and after your death, asleep, you escape from the graveyard or cemetery... Miserable specter! Wretched, soulless creature! Reflect and meditate. You must celebrate the great alliance of the Nineteenth Arcanum so that you can incarnate your soul and thus truly BE, because you, wretched creature, are not *being* yet. You are dreams. You die without knowing why and are born without knowing

FROM *Atalanta fugiens* by M. Maier, 1618

why. Only the blessed flame of love can make you truly exist, because you do not have a true existence yet.

Only with the Arcanum A.Z.F. can you engender your Christic vehicles. Your inner Buddha will be dressed with those vehicles first, thereafter your inner Christ. This is how you will become integral; you need to become integral.

Remember, good disciple, that now you are nothing but a sleeping specter and that your present internal vehicles are only mental formations that you must disintegrate, reduce to cosmic dust.

Be patient in the Great Work. If you want to incarnate your Inner Christ, then you must be sour like the lemon: be displeased; kill not only desire, but even the very shadow of desire. Be perfect in thought, word, and deed; be pure... pure... pure..!

The Philosophical Stone

Sex is represented by the Philosophical Stone; this is the Heliogabalus Stone.[126] The Elixir of Long Life cannot be acquired without this stone.

---

126 See glossary.

The two columns of the temple, Jakin and Boaz,[127] are the man and the woman who are in alliance in order to work with the Philosophical Stone. Whosoever finds the Philosophical Stone is transformed into a god.

The Great Tempter

The psychological "I" is the great tempter. The "I" hates Sexual Magic, because the "I" wants the complete satisfaction of desire. The "I" is the one who thinks and searches, whereas the Being does not need to think or search. When we are working in the Great Work, the "I" does not feel secure; thus, it searches for that which is called security. The students of the luminous path always fall into the abyss of perdition when searching for security. Therefore, do not allow yourself to be seduced by the great tempter. When the mind goes around searching for something, when the mind is searching for security, when the mind is looking for end results, it is because we are not prepared for the Great Work. Satan always goes around hunting for something; thus do not allow your mind to be poisoned by Satan. Do not waste your mental energy torpidly.

You waste your mental energy with the battle of reasoning; remember that your "I" is the one who reasons, whereas your soul does not need to reason. It is painful to see the specters of death reasoning about problems that do not exist. Sleeping specters are worthy of pity. Indeed, the "I" is the one who reasons.

Love

When the mind does not search anymore, when the mind does not search for refuge, when the mind does not go around coveting more books or knowledge, when the mind ignores the memories of desire, then only that which is called love will remain within us.

How great it is to love! Only the great souls can and know how to love.

---

127 The names of two symbolic pillars of the Temple of Solomon.

Arcanum 20

Let us now profoundly concentrate on the study of the Twentieth Arcanum of the Tarot. The hieroglyphics of this Arcanum are related to Judgment. As the angel is playing the trumpet, the dead are escaping from the graveyard. In this arcanum a man, a woman, and a child are resuscitating. This is a marvelous ternary.

ARCANUM 20 JUDGMENT
FROM THE TAROT
OF MARSEILLES

When studying this arcanum, we must not continue with the old Hebraic monotony; it is necessary for us to judiciously concentrate on the problem of resurrection if we truly want to be resurrected masters.[128]

Questions: How do we reach resurrection? How do we do not reach resurrection? How do we triumph? How do we fail?

Answers: We reach resurrection by working with the Arcanum A.Z.F., without spilling the cup of Hermes. We do not reach resurrection by spilling the cup of Hermes. When covetousness does not exist within us, we triumph; however, when covetousness exists within us, we fail.

Concrete explanation: there are two types of covetousness—the first type of covetousness is for money. The second type of covetousness is for psychic powers. Covetousness for money exists when we long for it for psychological purposes and not in order to acceptably take care of our physical necessities. Many people want money in order to gain social prestige, fame, high positions, etc. Covetousness for money does not exist when we get it with the sole purpose of taking care of our physical necessities. Thus, it is necessary to discover where necessity ends and where covetousness begins.

There is covetousness for psychic powers when we want end results. Those who only want end results are covetous. Those who go around here and there accumulating theories, search-

---

128 See glossary.

ing for powers, which today are in this school and tomorrow are in another, are in fact, bottled up within covetousness.

The mind that is bottled up within covetousness is unstable. It goes from lodge to lodge, from school to school, from sect to sect, always suffering, always longing for powers, light, wisdom, illumination, etc., without ever achieving anything since what is unstable can never comprehend that which is stable, permanent, and divine. Only God comprehends himself, thus the mind bottled up within the bottle of covetousness is incapable of comprehending the things that are not within the bottle.

Covetous people want to bottle up God. This is why they go around from school to school, always searching, always uselessly longing, because God cannot be bottled up by anybody.

Therefore, whosoever wants to work in the Great Work must first abandon covetousness. The stonemason who is covetous abandons the Great Work when he finds other work (even when the latter is indeed of darkness). Covetous people withdraw themselves from the Great Work. Many are they who start the work, yet few are those who finish it. The resurrected masters can be counted on the fingers of the hands.

Fatality

We knew the case of Jerome (who was a disciple of Cagliostro) who worked in the Great Work. This man acquired degrees, powers, initiations, tunics, capes, shrouds of distinction, a sword, etc.; thus, the progress of Jerome was worthy of admiration.

Everything went very well until the day he had the weak misfortune of revealing his intimate secret matters to an esotericist friend. This friend was horrified by the fact of not ejaculating the ens seminis and considered Jerome a barbarian. Thus, he advised Jerome to ejaculate the cup of Hermes; he instructed Jerome, telling him that in the supreme moment of orgasm, he must mentally assume an edifying and essentially dignified manner and thereafter, he said, "very saintly spill the cup of Hermes, and this is how one must work in the Great Work" (this is truly absurd logic).

Thus, the disciple of Count Cagliostro, Jerome (who indeed was not a strong man as was Cagliostro, the great Coptic) allowed himself to be convinced by absurd reasoning, and he spilled the sacred cup. Thus this is how he successively lost his shroud and sword, scepter and crown, tunics and degrees. This was fatality. Jerome was fulminated by the terrific ray of cosmic justice of the Sixteenth Arcanum.

Three Types of Resurrection

Thus, as there are three basic types of energy—masculine, feminine, and neutral—likewise, there are three types of resurrection. The first is the initiatic, spiritual resurrection. The second is the resurrection with the body of liberation. The third is the resurrection with the physical body. No one can pass through the second or through the third type of resurrection without having previously passed through the first, the spiritual resurrection.

Spiritual Resurrection

Spiritual resurrection is achieved only with initiation. We must first resurrect spiritually in the fire and thereafter in the light.

Resurrection with the Body of Liberation

The resurrection with the body of liberation[129] is achieved in the superior worlds. The body of liberation is organized with the best atoms of the physical body. This is a body of flesh that does not come from Adam; it is a body filled with indescribable beauty. The adepts can enter into the physical world and work in it with this paradisiacal body which they make visible and tangible by will.

---

129 See glossary.

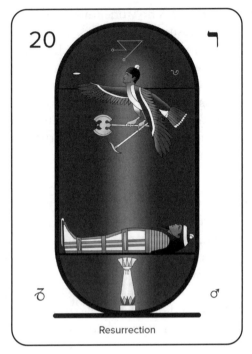

ARCANUM 20

RESURRECTION WITH THE PHYSICAL BODY

On the third day after his death, the adept comes (in his astral body) to the sepulcher, where his physical body lies. The master invokes his physical body and it obeys (by taking advantage of hyperspace and escapes from the sepulcher). This is how the sepulcher remains empty and the shroud left lying there. The body resurrects within the superior worlds. In the supersensible worlds, in hyperspace, holy women treat the body of the initiate with perfumes and aromatic ointments. Then, by obeying superior orders, the physical body penetrates within the master-soul, through the top of his sidereal head. This is how the master once again possesses his physical body. It is necessary to emphasize that in this type of resurrection, the physical body submerges itself within the supersensible worlds. When a resurrected master (whose body was within the holy sepulcher for three days) wants to enter into the physical world, he then exercises his willpower and can appear and disappear instantaneously, wherever he wants by will.

Jesus the Christ is a resurrected master that for three days had his physical body in the holy sepulcher. After the resurrection, Jesus appeared before the disciples (who were on their way to the village of Emmaus) and dined with them. After this, he was before the eleven apostles and before the unbelieving Thomas, who only believed when he put his fingers in the wounds of the holy body of the great master.

Hermes, Cagliostro, Paracelsus, Nicholas Flamel, Quetzalcoatl, St. Germain, Babaji, etc., preserved their physical bodies for thousands, and even millions of years, without death harming them. They are resurrected masters.

Elixir of Long Life

Only with the Arcanum A.Z.F. can the Elixir of Long Life be produced. Resurrection is impossible without the Elixir of Long Life.

Transmutation

ARCANUM 21

Arcanum 21

Let us now study the Twenty-first Arcanum of the Tarot. The hieroglyphic of this arcanum is the Fool.

When examining this arcanum, we perceive a wretched fool with a shoulder bag on a stick (within which he carries all of his absurdities and vices) and who as a rootless wanderer goes wandering aimlessly with no course or objective. His clothes in disarray leave his sexual organs exposed and a tiger cat, which is following him, bites him incessantly and he does not try to defend himself. So, sensitivity is found represented in this arcanum: the flesh, the material life.

ARCANUM 21 FROM THE TAROT OF MARSEILLES

We can also represent this arcanum with the inverted flaming star. Every initiate that allows himself to fall is indeed the Fool of the Tarot. As a matter of fact, when the alchemist spills the cup of Hermes, he is converted into the Fool of the Tarot.

It is necessary to annihilate desire if we want to avoid the danger of falling. Many masters who "swallowed soil" (many resurrected masters) fell and converted themselves into the Fool of the Twenty-first Arcanum of the Tarot. It is enough to remember Zanoni during the French Revolution; he was a resurrected master, and nonetheless he allowed himself to fall by falling in love with a female chorister from Naples. Zanoni died by the guillotine after having lived with the same physical body for thousands of years.

Whosoever wants to annihilate desire must discover its causes. The causes of desire are found in sensations. We live in a world of sensations and we need to comprehend them.

There are five types of sensations:
1. Visual sensations
2. Auditory sensations
3. Smell sensations
4. Taste sensations

5. Touch sensations

The five special types of sensations transform themselves into desire. Therefore, the causes of desire are found within sensations.

We must not condemn sensations, nor must we justify them. We need to profoundly comprehend them.

A pornographic image strikes the senses and then passes to the mind. The outcome of this perception is a sexual sensation that is soon transformed into animal desire. After passing through the sense of hearing and through the cerebral center of sensations, a vulgar morbid type of song is converted into sexual desire. We see a luxurious car, we sense it and thereafter we desire it. We taste a delicious cup of liqueur, we perceive its odor with our sense of smell and feel its delicious sensations, and thereafter we desire to drink more and more until we become inebriated. Thus, smell and taste turn us into gluttons and drunkards.

The sense of touch places itself under the service of all of our desires; thus this is how the "I" receives pleasure from amidst the vices and wanders like the Fool of the Tarot from life to life with his bag (within which he carries all of his vices and absurdities) on his shoulders.

Whosoever wants to annihilate desire, first of all needs to intellectually analyze the sensations and thereafter profoundly comprehend them. It is impossible to profoundly comprehend the contextual concept enclosed within a sensation with the mere intellect, since the intellect is just a small fraction of the mind. Therefore, if we want to comprehend the entire substantial context of a certain sensation (of any type) we then indispensably need the technique of internal meditation, because it is urgent to profoundly comprehend the "I" in all of the levels of the mind.

The mind has many layers, subconscious and unconscious levels that are normally unknown to humans. Many individuals who have achieved absolute chastity here in the physical world become terrible fornicators in other levels and profundities of the mind when they are submitted to difficult ordeals in the internal worlds. Great anchorites and hermit saints discovered with horror that the Fool of the Tarot continued alive in other more profound levels of their understanding. Indeed, only by comprehending the sensations in all the creases of the mind can we annihilate desire and kill the Fool of the Tarot (who hides himself within all of those creases of our mind).

It is necessary for our students to learn how to see and hear without translating. When a man perceives the beautiful figure of a woman and commits the error of translating that perception into the language of his sexual desires, then the outcome is sexual desire; this type of desire, even when it is forgotten, continues living internally in other unconscious levels of the mind. Thus, this is how the "I" incessantly fornicates in the internal worlds. Therefore, it is important to learn how to see without translating, to see without judging. It is indispensable to see, hear, taste, smell, and touch with creative comprehension. Thus, just like this, we can annihilate the causes of desire. Indeed the tree of desire has roots that we must study and profoundly comprehend.

Upright perception and creative comprehension annihilate the causes of desire; this is how the mind escapes from the bottle of desire and is elevated unto the superior worlds, then the awakening of the consciousness arrives.

Normally, the mind is found bottled up within the bottle of desire; thus, it is indispensable to take the mind out of the bottle if indeed what we want is the awakening of the consciousness. To awaken the consciousness is impossible without taking the mind out of its bottled up condition.

We constantly hear complaints from many students who suffer because during the slumber of their physical bodies they live unconscious within the superior worlds. Many of them have performed esoteric practices in order to achieve astral projection, yet they do not succeed. When we study the life of these whiners, we discover within them the Fool of the Tarot; these people are full of desires.

We kill desire only by comprehending sensations. Only by annihilating desire can the mind that is normally bottled up within desire be liberated. The awakening of the consciousness is produced only by liberating the mind from desire.

The Fool of the Tarot is the psychological "I", "the myself," the reincorporating ego.

If we want to end the causes of desire, then we need to live in a state of constant vigilance. It is urgent to live in a state of alert perception, alert novelty.

The "I" is a big book, a book of many volumes, and only by means of the technique of internal meditation can we study this book.

When we discover and profoundly comprehend a defect in all of the levels of the mind, then it is completely disintegrated. Each time a defect is disintegrated, something new occupies its place: an esoteric password, a mantra, a cosmic initiation, an esoteric degree, a secret power, etc. Thus, this is how, little by little, we fill ourselves with true wisdom.

The kabbalistic addition of this arcanum gives us the following outcome: 2 + 1 = 3. One is the Father (Kether), two is the Son (Chokmah), three is the Holy Spirit (Binah): they are the resplendent dragon of wisdom within any human being that comes into the world. Anyone who achieves the dissolution of the psychological "I" (the Fool of the Tarot) incarnates one's resplendent dragon of wisdom. Whosoever incarnates the resplendent dragon of wisdom becomes a spirit of wisdom.

> *"Speak not in the ears of a fool: for he will despise the wisdom of thy words."* —Proverbs 23:9

Coexistence

It is not by isolating ourselves from our fellowmen that we will discover our defects. It is only by means of coexistence that we discover ourselves. Thus, by means of coexisting with others, we surprisingly discover our defects, because they flourish and spring forth from within and emerge to the external world by means of our human personality. Thus, in social coexistence are self-discovery and self-revelation.

When we discover a defect, we must first intellectually analyze it, and thereafter comprehend it in all of the inner layers of the mind, by means of the technique of meditation.

It is necessary to focus on the discovered defect and meditate on it with the intention of comprehending it profoundly.

Meditation must be combined with the slumber state.[130]
Thus, this is how, by means of profound vision, we become
cognizant of the defect that we are trying to comprehend.
Thus once the defect is dissolved, "something new" arrives to
us. It is necessary to be in a state of alert perception and alert
novelty during internal meditation.

In order to receive that "something new," a defect must be
replaced by it; a defect must be substituted for it. Thus, this is
how the human being becomes truly wise; this is the path of
wisdom.

Intuition

While we are dissolving the Fool of the Twenty-first
Arcanum of the Tarot, intuition is being developed within.
Intuition is the flower of intelligence. Intuition and comprehension replace reasoning and desire, since these are attributes
of the "I." Intuition allows us to penetrate into the past, into
the present, and into the future. Intuition allows us to penetrate into the deep meaning of all things.

Intuition grants us entrance into the world of the ineffable
gods. Any intuitive initiate converts into a true prophet.

Practice for the Development of Intuition

It is urgent for the devotee of the path of the razor's edge
to intensify the development of intuition. This faculty resides
in the coronary chakra. This chakra shines upon the pineal
gland, which is the seat of the soul, the third eye. Modern
scientists believe that they know more than the ancient sages

---

130 "Meditation must be combined intelligently with concentration and
drowsiness. Concentration mixed with drowsiness produces enlightenment. Many esotericists think that meditation in no way should be
combined with the drowsiness of the body, but those who think that
way are wrong, because meditation without drowsiness ruins the brain.
Always use sleep in combination with the technique of meditation, but a
controlled sleep... We must "ride" on sleep, and not let the sleep ride on
us." —Samael Aun Weor, The Conquest of the Illuminating Void

from the ancient school of mysteries; thus, they deny all of these esoteric matters related with the pineal gland and take it only to the purely physiological side (with this, pretending to strike the faces of the great hierophants with a white glove). Notwithstanding, the ancient sages from old times never ignore that the pineal gland is a small, reddish-gray cone-shaped tissue located in the center of the brain. The old sages knew very well that the hormone that is secreted by this gland is intimately related with the development of the sexual organs, and that after maturity, this gland degenerates into fibered tissues that no longer secrete that hormone, and then impotence arrives. There is an exception to this process, and this is known only by the Gnostics.[131]

Gnostics preserve the activity of their pineal gland, and its sexual, functional secretion remains active by means of Sexual Magic throughout their entire life. The pineal gland is the center of intuitive polyvoyance. Intuition manifests within the heart as presentments; yet, in the pineal gland such presentments are converted into intuitive images.

It is urgent for our devotees to practice the powerful mantra of intuition. This mantra is the following: **Triiiinnnnn**... prolong the sound of the vowel "I" and of the consonant "N," it sounds like a bell. The student submerged within a perfect meditation with the mind empty must be inundated by silence, and then must mentally vocalize the sacred mantra. This mantra can be chanted as many times as one wishes to do so. After about ten minutes of vocalization, the student must cease vocalizing the mantra and continue with the mind empty for an indefinite period of time. When the great silence inundates us, then the experience of the great Reality comes.

---

131 Gnostics are those who have gnosis, conscious experience. Such persons come from every religion in the world.

Arcanum 22

Let us now study the Twenty-second Arcanum of Kabbalah. This arcanum is the Crown of Life.

Revelation 2:10 states:

"Be thou faithful unto death, and I will give thee a crown of life."

To find faithful people in these studies is difficult. All those who enter into Gnosis want to develop esoteric powers immediately; this is grave. People believe that the path of the realization of the inner Self is like playing football or like playing tennis. People have still not learned how to be serious. Commonly, people enter into these studies with the longing of acquiring powers within a few months. However, when they realize that they need patience and hard work, they then desperately leave in search of another school. Thus, this is how they waste their life away, fleeing from one school to the next, from one lodge to another, from institution to institution, until they get old and die without ever having achieved anything. Thus, this is how humanity is.

One can count those who are truly serious and truly prepared for the practical adepthood on the fingers of the hands.

Beloved disciples, you need to develop each of the twenty-two major arcana of the Tarot within yourselves. You are *imitatus*, or rather, one who others have put on the path of the razor's edge. Exert yourself to become *adeptus*, one who is the product of one's own deeds, the one that conquers science by his own, the child of one's own work.

Primeval Gnosis teaches three steps through which anyone who works in the flaming forge of Vulcan has to pass. These steps are as follows:

1. Purification

2. Illumination

3. Perfection

The Return

ARCANUM 22

It so happens that curious people who enter into our Gnostic studies want immediate illumination, astral projection, clairvoyance, practical magic, etc., and when they do not achieve this, they immediately leave.

No one can achieve illumination without having been previously purified. Only those that have achieved purification and sanctity can enter into the hall of illumination.

There are also many students that enter into our studies purely out of curiosity. They want to be wise immediately. Paul of Tarsus stated:

> *"We speak wisdom among them that are perfect."*
> —1 Corinthians 2:6

Therefore, only those who achieve the third step are perfect. Only among them can divine wisdom be spoken of.

In the ancient Egypt of the Pharaohs, among the esoteric Masons, the three steps of the path were:

1. Apprentice

2. Companion

3. Master

Candidates remained in the degree of apprentice for seven years, and sometimes longer. Only when the hierophants were completely sure of the purification and sanctity of those candidates would they then pass them to the second step.

The first faculty that the candidate develops is the one related with the degree of listener, the faculty of clairaudience (esoteric hearing).

Indeed, illumination begins only after seven years of apprenticeship. Nevertheless, students believe that spiritual faculties are going to be immediately developed, and when they realize that this subject matter is serious, they flee. This is the sad reality; this is why in life it is very rare to find someone who is prepared for adepthood.

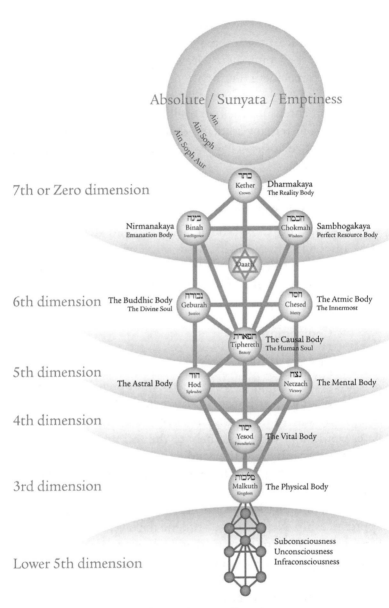

THE CROWN OF LIFE ON THE TREE OF LIFE

The Crown of Life is formed by the first trinity, at the top:
Kether (Hebrew: "Crown"), Chokmah (Wisdom) and
Binah (Intelligence).

The Crown of Life

The Innermost is not the Crown of Life. The Crown of Life has three profundities, and these are beyond the Innermost. The Crown of Life is our resplendent dragon of wisdom, our inner Christ.

The Three Profundities

The first profundity is the origin of life, the second is the origin of the word, and the third is the origin of the sexual force. These three profundities of the resplendent dragon of wisdom are beyond the Innermost.

The Innermost must be sought within the unknowable profundities of oneself.

The Number 22

The three profundities of the resplendent dragon of wisdom emanated from a mathematical point: this is the Ain Soph, the interior Atomic Star that has always smiled upon us. The Holy Trinity emanated from this Inner Star. The three profundities will return, they will fuse together again with this Inner Star.

The number 22 is kabbalistically added as follows: 2 + 2 = 4.

The Holy Three emanates from the Inner Star, thus, the Holy Trinity plus its Inner Star is the Holy Four, the mysterious Tetragrammaton, which is יהוה Iod-Hei-Vav-Hei. Now we comprehend why the Twenty-second Arcanum is the Crown of Life.

יהוה

"Be thou faithful unto death, and I will give thee a crown of life." —Revelation 2:10

Blessed be the one who incarnates the spirit of wisdom (Chokmah).

Those Buddhas who do not renounce Nirvana can never incarnate the Cosmic Christ, who is beyond the inner Buddha. Our inner Buddha has to seek the Cosmic Christ within its own unknowable profundities. The Cosmic Christ is the Glorian, the incessant eternal breath profoundly unknowable to itself, the ray that joins us to the abstract absolute space.

Hieroglyph

Hieroglyphics of this arcanum: the crown of life is amidst the four mysterious animals of sexual alchemy. In the middle of the crown, truth is represented as a naked woman who has a little stick in each hand (the priest and the priestess); this is sexual alchemy. We can incarnate the truth only by working in the flaming forge of Vulcan

ARCANUM 21 FROM THE
TAROT OF MARSEILLES

The Ark of Alliance

The Ark of Alliance[132] had four Cherubim (two at each end); with the tips of their wings they touched each other and were found in the sexual position (a man and woman copulating). The blossoming staff of Aaron, the Cup or Omer containing the Manna, and the two tablets of the law were within the Ark; these elements are four, as four is the outcome of the addition of 22 (2+2=4).

The Internal Lodge

The first duty of any Gnostic is to be sure that the lodge is protected. During the degree of apprentice, attention is focused on the astral plane. Thus, the inner lodge must be protected. The astral body must be clean from any type of animal passions and desire.

In the second degree, the mental lodge must be protected. Thus, worldly thoughts must be cast out of the temple. It is necessary to protect the inner lodge very well so that doctrines,

---

132 The Ark of the Covenant described by Moses.

people, demons, etc. do not penetrate inside the inner sanctuary and thus sabotage the Great Work. We have witnessed (apparently very serious) students who became careless, who did not know how to protect their inner lodge, and were thus invaded by people and strange doctrines. Most of the time, these careless students continued their work in the flaming forge of Vulcan, but they combined it with very different methods and systems. Thus, the outcome of all of this was a true Tower of Babel, a barbaric confusion whose only purpose was to bring disorder into the inner lodge of their consciousness.

Therefore, it is necessary to have the inner lodge, the authentic school of inner education, in perfect order. We are absolutely sure that there is only one door and only one way: sex. Thus, anything that is not through this way is just a miserable waste of time.

We are not against any religion, school, sect, order, etc. Nonetheless, we firmly know that inside our individual inner lodge we must have order, so that we avoid confusion and error.

• • •

We have accomplished this charge and feel satisfaction, since we have served humanity and ourselves.

To present a work of such magnitude encourages us and prepares us for new services.

Humanity has never liked the doctrine of the Gnostics. Hence, the substantial content of this work is for a more advanced humanity, because the people of this barbaric epoch are not capable of understanding these things.

We hope that you, friend, as a good reader, know how to find the happiness, joy, and peace that we want for all beings within this treasure that you now hold in your hands. If however, you despise it, it is because you cannot find anything that entices you within it. But do not be selfish, think about the one who is next to you that might need it, and give the book to them.

May your Father who is in secret and may your Divine Mother Kundalini bless you.

APPENDICES

Glossary

Alchemy: Al (as a connotation of the Arabic word Allah: al-, the + ilah, God) means "The God." Also Al (Hebrew) for "highest" or El "God." Chem or Khem is from kimia (Greek) which means "to fuse or cast a metal." Also from Khem, the ancient name of Egypt. The synthesis is Al-Kimia: "to fuse with the highest" or "to fuse with God."

Arcanum: (Latin. plural: arcana). A secret or mystery known only to the specially educated. The root of the term "ark" as in the Ark of Noah and the Ark of the Covenent.

Arcanum A.Z.F.: The practice of sexual transmutation as couple (male-female), a technique known in Tantra and Alchemy. Arcanum refers to a hidden truth or law. A.Z.F. stands for A (agua, water), Z (azufre, sulfur), F (fuego, fire), and is thus: water + fire = consciousness. . Also, A (azoth = chemical element that refers to fire). A & Z are the first and last letters of the alphabet thus referring to the Alpha & Omega (beginning & end).

Archaeus: From Ancient Greek ἀρχαῖος (arkhaîos, "original, ancient"). Compare with Arche (Ancient Greek: ἀρχή; "beginning", "origin" or "source of action") + Chaos (Ancient Greek: χάος, romanized: kháos), the void, the Absolute. In alchemy, archeus refers to the vital principle or force that presides over the growth and continuation of living beings; the anima mundi or malleable power of the alchemists and philosophers. See also: astral light.

"If [the alchemist] will do wonders with Christ, and tincture the corrupt body to the new-birth, he must first be baptized [through chastity], and then he gets an hunger after God's bread [knowledge], and this hunger has in it the verbum fiat, viz. the archeus to the new generation, that is, the Mercury: But I do not speak here of a priest's baptism; the artist must understand it magically; God and man must first come together ere thou baptizest, as it came to pass in Christ: The Deity first entered into the humanity, but the humanity could not presently comprehend it, till it was quickened through baptism [chastity], and the hunger, viz. the dead Mercury in the human essence, was again stirred up in the heavenly part." —Jakob Boehme (17th cent)

Astral: This term is dervied from "pertaining to or proceeding from the stars," but in the esoteric knowledge it refers to the emotional aspect of the fifth dimension, which in Hebrew is called Hod.

Astral Body: The body utilized by the consciousness in the fifth dimension or world of dreams. What is commonly called the Astral Body is not the true Astral Body, it is rather the Lunar Protoplasmatic Body, also known as the Kama Rupa (Sanskrit, "body of desires") or "dream body" (Tibetan rmi-lam-gyi lus). The true Astral Body is Solar (being superior to Lunar Nature) and must be created, as the Master Jesus indicated in the Gospel of John 3:5-6, "Except a man be born of water and of the Spirit, he cannot enter into the kingdom of God. That which is born of the flesh is flesh; and that which is born of the Spirit is spirit." The Solar Astral Body is created as a result of the Third Initiation of Major Mysteries (Serpents of Fire), and is perfected in the Third Serpent of Light. In Tibetan Buddhism, the Solar Astral Body is known as the illusory body (sgyu-lus). This body is related to the emotional center and to the sephirah Hod.

"Really, only those who have worked with the Maithuna (White Tantra) for many years can possess the Astral Body." —Samael Aun Weor, *The Elimination of Satan's Tail*

Astral World: The emotional aspect of the fifth dimension, which in Hebrew is called Hod. When we dream, our consciousness wanders asleep in the astral world, repeating its daily activities. Ruled by the Moon.

"The astral world is governed by the Moon. This is why astral projections become easier during the crescent moon and a little bit more arduous during the waning moon... Hod, the astral world, is governed by the Moon, but many Kabbalists suppose that it is governed by Mercury, and they are mistaken." —Samael Aun Weor, *Tarot and Kabbalah*

Atalanta: Greek atalantos "having the same value (as a man)," from a- "one, together" + talanton "balance, weight, value." Atalanta is a symbol from Greek mythology whose tale is beautifully told in Ovid's Metamorphoses, and is also the basis of the landmark multimedia alchemical opus Atalanta fugiens by Michael Maier.

"The innocent cause of so much sorrow was a maiden whose face you might truly say was boyish for a girl, yet too girlish for a boy. Her fortune had been told, and it was to this effect: "Atalanta, do not marry; marriage will be your ruin." Terrified by this oracle, she fled the society of men, and devoted herself to the sports of the chase. To all suitors (for she had many) she imposed a condition which was generally effectual in relieving her of their persecutions- "I will be the prize of him who shall conquer me in the race; but death must be the penalty of all who try and fail." In spite of this hard condition some would try. Hippomenes was to be judge of the race. "Can it be possible that any will be so rash as to risk so much for a wife?" said he. But when he saw her lay aside her robe for the race, he changed his mind, and said, "Pardon me, youths, I knew not the prize you were competing for." As he surveyed them he wished them all to be beaten, and swelled with envy of any one that seemed at all likely to win. While such were his thoughts, the virgin darted forward. As she ran she looked more beautiful than ever. The breezes seemed to give wings to her feet; her hair flew over her shoulders, and the gay fringe of her garment fluttered behind her. A ruddy hue tinged the whiteness of her skin, such as a crimson curtain casts on a marble wall. All her competitors were distanced, and were put to death without mercy. Hippomenes, not daunted by this result, fixing his eyes on the virgin, said, "Why boast of beating those laggards? I offer myself for the contest." Atalanta looked at him with a pitying countenance, and hardly knew whether she would rather conquer him or not. "What god can tempt one so young and handsome to throw himself away?

I pity him, not for his beauty (yet he is beautiful), but for his youth. I wish he would give up the race, or if he will be so mad, I hope he may outrun me." While she hesitates, revolving these thoughts, the spectators grow impatient for the race, and her father prompts her to prepare. Then Hippomenes addressed a prayer to Venus: "Help me, Venus, for you have led me on." Venus heard and was propitious. In the garden of her temple, in her own island of Cyprus, is a tree with yellow leaves and yellow branches and golden fruit. Hence she gathered three golden apples, and unseen by any one else, gave them to Hippomenes, and told him how to use them. The signal is given; each starts from the goal and skims over the sand. So light their tread, you would almost have thought they might run over the river surface or over the waving grain without sinking. The cries of the spectators cheered Hippomenes,- "Now, now, do your best! haste, haste! you gain on her! relax not! one more effort!" It was doubtful whether the youth or the maiden heard these cries with the greater pleasure. But his breath began to fail him, his throat was dry, the goal yet far off. At that moment be threw down one of the golden apples. The virgin was all amazement. She stopped to pick it up. Hippomenes shot ahead. Shouts burst forth from all sides. She redoubled her efforts, and soon overtook him. Again he threw an apple. She stopped again, but again came up with him. The goal was near; one chance only remained. "Now, goddess," said he, "prosper your gift!" and threw the last apple off at one side. She looked at it, and hesitated; Venus impelled her to turn aside for it. She did so, and was vanquished. The youth carried off his prize. But the lovers were so full of their own happiness that they forgot to pay due honour to Venus; and the goddess was provoked at their ingratitude. She caused them to give offence to Cybele [compelled by lust, they had sex in the temple of the goddess]. That powerful goddess was not to be insulted with impunity. She took from them their human form and turned them into animals of characters resembling their own: of the huntress-heroine, triumphing in the blood of her lovers, she made a lioness, and of her lord and master a lion, and yoked them to her car [chariot], where they are still to be seen in all representations, in statuary or painting, of the goddess Cybele." — Thomas Bulfinch [1855]

Atoms: While modern science studies atoms as the basic unit of matter, they are ignoring the two other essential aspects of each atom: energy and consciousness.

"Every atom is a trio of matter, energy and consciousness. The consciousness of every atom is always an intelligent elemental. If the materialists are not capable of seeing those elementals, it is because they still do not know the scientific procedures that allow us to see them. We have special methods in order to see those creatures. Indeed, the atom is a truly infinitely small planetary system. Those planetary systems of the atoms are formed by ultra-atomic ternaries that spin around their centers of gravitation. The atom with its Alpha, Beta, and Gamma rays is a trio of matter, energy and consciousness. " —Samael Aun Weor, *Sexology, the Basis of Endocrinology and Criminology*

Thus understood as being more than mere matter, atoms have great significance for all living creatures, since atoms form the basis for all living things. That is why the spiritual classic The Dayspring of Youth by M explains that atoms are "Minute bodies of intelligence possessing the dual attributes of Nature and man." While there are many types and levels of such atomic intelligences, both positive and negative, some of particular importance are Aspiring atoms, Destructive atoms, the Nous atom, Informer atoms, Scholar atoms, etc.

"Life will not be fully understood until we recognise the living forces within us and transplant atoms of a higher nature into the body. This will eventually help humanity to become the personification of justice. Our atomic centres are similar to the starry clusters in the sky, and each atom is a minute intelligence revolving within its own atmosphere. When we aspire we unite ourselves to atoms that have preceded us in evolution; for they evolve as we evolve: this body being their university, and they prepare the path for us to follow." —*The Dayspring of Youth* by M

"The atom of the Father is situated in the root of the nose; this is the atom of willpower. The seven serpents ascend by means of willpower, by dominating the animal impulse. The atom of the Father is situated in the root of the nose; this is the atom of willpower. The seven serpents ascend by means of willpower, by dominating the animal impulse. The atom of the Son is in the pituitary gland, whose exponent is the Nous atom (the Son of Man) in the heart. The angelic atom of the Holy Spirit shines in the pineal gland, within the chakra Sahasrara. The atom of the Father governs or controls the right ganglionary chord Pingala within which the solar atoms, the positive force, ascends. The atom of the Son governs the Sushumna canal, within which the neutral forces ascend. The atom of the Holy Spirit governs the Ida canal, within which the negative forces ascend. This is why it is related with our creative sexual forces and with the rays of the moon, which are intimately related with the reproduction of the races. Each of the seven chakras from the spinal medulla is governed by an angelic atom." —Samael Aun Weor, *Kabbalah of the Mayan Mysteries*

Azoth: In alchemy, Azoth is the life principle of all metals. Azoth is most known in relation to Paracelsus.

"The Azoth and the fire clean the brass, that is to say, they clean and completely remove all of its blackness." —Villanova, *Semita Semitae*

It is commonly stated that the word Azoth is derived from Arabic al-zā'ūq: "the mercury." While this is relevant, it is not the only important appearance of this word.

"Behold now, observe תאזח Hazoth (the Azoth) is near, flee to it, and it is small: I pray thee, let me escape thither -- is it not small? -- and my soul shall live." —Genesis 19: 20

"And Adam said, זאת zo'th [is] now bone of my bones, and flesh of my flesh: זאת zo'th shall be called אשה 'ishshah, because זאת zo'th was taken out of שיא 'iysh." —Genesis 2:23

זאת + שיא = Ish-Zoth = Azoth.

"...Sulphur, Mercury, and Salt, which, volatized and fixed alternately, compose the AZOTH..." —Eliphas Levi, *Transcendental Magic* (1856)

"...the four elements of Alchemy are: Salt, Mercury, Sulfur, and Azoth: the Salt is the matter; the Mercury is the Ens Seminis, the Azoth is the mysterious ray of Kundalini . " —Samael Aun Weor, *Alchemy and Kabbalah in the Tarot*

"Whosoever wants to edify the New Jerusalem must first awaken the sacred fire of Kundalini . This Pentecostal serpent is INRI, Azoth." —Samael Aun Weor, *The Aquarian Message*

"The Mercury is the metallic soul of the sperm; understand, it is the metallic soul . Allow me to illustrate this better: there are three types of Mercury. The first Mercury is called the Brute Azoth or the sperm. The second Mercury is called the metallic soul of the sperm, and the third Mercury is called Mercury plus Sulfur (Mercury fecundated by fire). To conclude, the Mercury is the metallic soul of the sperm, and the Sulfur is the sacred fire." —Samael Aun Weor, *The Major Mysteries*

"The name of א Aleph and the sacred name of ת Thau must be uttered, united in the Kabbalistic name of Azoth... Sophia is found in the sexual Chaos, in the brute Azoth. We must liberate Sophia from within the darkness of the Chaos... The brute Azoth, which is the sacred sperm not yet worked with, is a closed book. We need to open that book." —Samael Aun Weor, *The Gnostic Bible: The Pistis Sophia Unveiled*

Alchemists always address three symbolic substances: mercury, sulfur, and salt. Azoth is added as a fourth, mysterious permuting life principle. According to Alchemy: Salt, sulfur, and mercury each have a triune nature, for each of these substances contain, in reality, also the other two substances. Therefore, the body of Salt is threefold: salt, sulfur, and mercury; but in the body of Salt one of the three (salt) predominates. Mercury is likewise composed of salt, sulfur, and mercury with the latter element predominating. Sulfur, similarly, is indeed salt, sulfur, and mercury, with sulfur predominating. The permutation of these nine divisions —3 times 3 - 9 is done thanks to Azoth, the sacred fire of Kundalini . Azoth is therefore the universal substance, the invisible eternal fire, electricity, magnetism, astral light, the measureless spirit of life, the fiery mercurial essence that flows out from the throne of God and the Lamb, the spinal medulla. This is the River of living water in Eden – Sex, the Genesiac mist of the earth, the igneous particles 'Haishim' within the dust of the ground (Adamah) from where God formed the electronic bodies of Adam, the true human being.

Bodhisattva: (Sanskrit) Literally, the Sankrit term Bodhi means enlightenment or wisdom, while Sattva means essence or goodness; therefore, the term Bodhisattva literally means "essence of wisdom." The Tibetan translation of this word is jangchub sempa. Jangchub (Sanskrit bodhi) means enlightenment, and sempa (Sanskrit sattva) means hero or a being, therefore meaning "enlightened hero." The word jangchub is from jang, "the overcoming and elimination of all obstructive forces," and chub, "realization of full knowledge." Sempa is a reference to great compassion. The 14th Dalai Lama said, "...bodhisattvas are beings who, out of intense compassion, never shift their attention away from sentient beings; they are purpetually concerned for the welfare of all beings, and they dedicate themselves entirely to securing that welfare. Thus the very name bodhisattva indicates a being who, through wisdom, heroically focuses on the attainment of enlightenment out of compassionate concern for all beings. The word itself conveys the key qualities of such an infinitely altruistic being."

"We, the bodhisattvas of compassion who love humanity immensely, state: as long as there is a single tear in any human eye, as long as there is even one suffering heart, we refuse to accept the happiness of Nirvana... We must seek the means to become more and more useful to this wretched, suffering humanity." —Samael Aun Weor, *The Major Mysteries*

In the esoteric or secret teachings of Tibet and Gnosticism, a Bodhisattva is a human being who has reached the Fifth Initiation of Fire (Tiphereth) and has chosen to continue working by means of the Straight Path, renouncing the easier Spiral Path (in Nirvana), and returning instead to help suffering humanity. By means of this sacrifice, this individual incarnates the Christ (Avalokitesvara), thereby embodying the supreme source of wisdom and compassion. This is the entrance to the Direct Path to complete liberation from the ego, a route that only very few take, due to the fact that one must pay the entirety of one's karma in one life. Those who have taken this road have been the most remarkable figures in human history: Jesus, Buddha, Mohamed, Krishna, Moses, Padmasambhava, Milarepa, Joan of Arc, Fu-Ji, and many others whose names are not remembered or known. Of course, even among bodhisattvas there are many levels of Being: to be a bodhisattva does not mean that one is enlightened. Interestingly, the Christ in Hebrew is called Chokmah, which means "wisdom," and in Sanskrit the same is Vishnu, the root of the word "wisdom." It is Vishnu who sent his Avatars into the world in order to guide humanity. These avatars were Krishna, Buddha, Rama, and the Avatar of this age: the Avatar Kalki.

"The truly humble Bodhisattva never praises himself. The humble Bodhisattva says, 'I am just a miserable slug from the mud of the earth, I am a nobody. My person has no value. The work is what is worthy.' The Bodhisattva is the human soul of a Master. The Master is the internal God." —Samael Aun Weor, *The Aquarian Message*

"Let it be understood that a Bodhisattva is a seed, a germ, with the possibility of transcendental, divine development by means of pressure coming from the Height." —Samael Aun Weor, *The Gnostic Bible: The Pistis Sophia Unveiled*

Body of Liberation: The perfected body of a highly developed master. In Sanskrit, this body is called Svabhavikakaya.

"The Body of Liberation has a Christic appearance. It exudes the aroma of perfection. This body replaces the physical body; it is made of flesh, but it is not the born from the flesh of Adam. This is the body of paradisiacal beings; this body is not submitted to illnesses or death." —Samael Aun Weor, *The Major Mysteries*

"We extract the body of liberation from the physical body. This body is made with flesh, but flesh that does not come from Adam. It is a body filled with millenarian perfections. It is elaborated with the most evolved atoms of our physical body. [...] The body of Liberation is neither subjected to sickness, nor to death. The body of Liberation is made with flesh and bones, but it is flesh that does not come from Adam. It is flesh from the Cosmic-Christ. The body of Liberation is similar to the Divine Rabbi of Galilee. The body of Liberation is the body of the Gods." —Samael Aun Weor, *Treatise of Sexual Alchemy*

"The body of liberation converts us into citizens of Eden." —Samael Aun Weor, *Igneous Rose*

Buddha: Literally, "awakened one." One of the Three Jewels (Tri-ratna). Commonly used to refer simply to the Buddha Shakyamuni (the "founder" of Buddhism), the term Buddha is actually a title. There are a vast number of Buddhas, each at different levels of attainment. At the ultimate level, a Buddha is a being who has become totally free of suffering. The Inner Being (Chesed) first becomes a Buddha when the Human Soul completes the work of the Fourth Initiation of Fire (related to Netzach, the mental body).

Centers, Seven: The human being has seven centers of psychological activity. The first five are the intellectual, emotional, motor, instinctive, and sexual centers. However, through inner development one learns how to utilize the superior emotional and superior intellectual centers. Most people do not use these two at all.

Chakra: (Sanskrit) Literally, "wheel." The chakras are subtle centers of energetic transformation. There are hundreds of chakras in our hidden physiology, but seven primary ones related to the awakening of consciousness.

"The chakras are centres of Shakti as vital force... The chakras are not perceptible to the gross senses. Even if they were perceptible in the living body which they help to organise, they disappear with the disintegration of organism at death." —Swami Sivananda, *Kundalini Yoga*

"The chakras are points of connection through which the divine energy circulates from one to another vehicle of the human being." —Samael Aun Weor, *Aztec Christic Magic*

Christ: Derived from the Greek Christos, "the Anointed One," and Krestos, whose esoteric meaning is "fire." The word Christ is a title, not a personal name.

"Indeed, Christ is a Sephirothic Crown (Kether, Chokmah and Binah) of incommensurable wisdom, whose purest atoms shine within Chokmah, the world of the Ophanim. Christ is not the Monad, Christ is not the Theosophical Septenary; Christ is not the Jivan-Atman. Christ is the Central Sun. Christ is the ray that unites us to the Absolute." —Samael Aun Weor, *Tarot and Kabbalah*

"The Gnostic Church adores the saviour of the world, Jesus. The Gnostic Church knows that Jesus incarnated Christ, and that is why they adore him. Christ is not a human nor a divine individual. Christ is a title given to all fully self-realized masters. Christ is the Army of the Voice. Christ is the Verb. The Verb is far beyond the body, the soul and the Spirit. Everyone who is able to incarnate the Verb receives in fact the title of Christ. Christ is the Verb itself. It is necessary for everyone of us to incarnate the Verb (Word). When the Verb becomes flesh in us we speak with the verb of light. In actuality, several masters have incarnated the Christ. In secret India, the Christ Yogi Babaji has lived for millions of years; Babaji is immortal. The great master of wisdom Kout Humi also incarnated the Christ. Sanat Kumara, the founder of the great College of Initiates of the White Lodge, is another living Christ. In the past, many incarnated the Christ. In the present, some have incarnated the Christ. In the future many will incarnate the Christ. John the Baptist also incarnated the Christ. John the Baptist is a living Christ. The difference between Jesus and the other masters that also incarnated the Christ has to do with hierarchy. Jesus is the highest Solar initiate of the cosmos..." —Samael Aun Weor, *The Perfect Matrimony*

Comprehension: From Latin comprehensionem, "to seize, to get hold of." Similar to Sanskrit: vid, manas jna, "to know." Tibetan: go.

"To comprehend is something immediate, direct, something that we vividly undergo intensely, something that we experience very profoundly, and which inevitably becomes the true intimate source of conscious action. To remember or to recollect is something dead, something that belongs to the past, and that unfortunately becomes an ideal, a motto, an idea, an idealism that we want to mechanically imitate and unconsciously follow. In true comprehension, in profound comprehension, in intimate in-depth comprehension, there exists only the intimate pressure of the consciousness, a persistent pressure born from the Essence that we carry within, and that is all. Authentic comprehension is manifested as a spontaneous, natural, and simple action, free from the depressing process of selection; it is pure, without any type of indecision." —Samael Aun Weor, *Fundamentals of Gnostic Education*

"Knowledge and comprehension are different. Knowledge is of the mind. Comprehension is of the heart." —Samael Aun Weor, *Treatise of Revolutionary Psychology*

"The annihilation of the psychic aggregates can be made possible only by radically comprehending our errors through meditation and by the evident Self-reflection of the Being... It is urgent to know how to meditate, in order to comprehend any psychic aggregate, or in other words, any psychological defect. It is indispensable to know how to work with all our heart and with all our soul, if we want the elimination to occur." —Samael Aun Weor, *The Gnostic Bible: The Pistis Sophia Unveiled*

"[The Apostle] Thomas is the part of the Being who is related with the intimate sense of comprehension. A great deal of analysis, reflection, and above all, meditation and evident self-reflection of the Being are indispensable for comprehension." —Samael Aun Weor, *The Gnostic Bible: The Pistis Sophia Unveiled*

"No phenomena of nature can be integrally comprehended if we consider it isolated." —Samael Aun Weor, *The Revolution of the Dialectic*

Consciousness: "Wherever there is life, there is consciousness. Consciousness is inherent to life as humidity is inherent to water." —Samael Aun Weor, Sexology, the Basis of Endocrinology and Criminology

From various dictionaries: 1. The state of being conscious; knowledge of one's own existence, condition, sensations, mental operations, acts, etc. 2. Immediate knowledge or perception of the presence of any object, state, or sensation. 3. An alert cognitive state in which you are aware of yourself and your situation. In universal Gnosticism, the range of potential consciousness is allegorized in the Ladder of Jacob, upon which the angels ascend and descend. Thus there are higher and lower levels of consciousness, from the level of demons at the bottom, to highly realized angels in the heights.

"It is vital to understand and develop the conviction that consciousness has the potential to increase to an infinite degree." —The 14th Dalai Lama

"Light and consciousness are two phenomena of the same thing; to a lesser degree of consciousness, corresponds a lesser degree of light; to a greater degree of consciousness, a greater degree of light." —Samael Aun Weor, *The Esoteric Treatise of Hermetic Astrology*

Devi: "DEVI or Maheswari or Parasakti is the Supreme Sakti or Power of the Supreme Being. When Vishnu and Mahadeva destroyed various Asuras, the power of Devi was behind them. Devi took Brahma, Vishnu, and Rudra and gave them necessary Sakti to proceed with the work of creation, preservation, and destruction. Devi is the Creatrix of the universe. She is the Universal Mother. Durga, Kali, Bhagavati, Bhavani, Ambal, Ambika, Jagadamba, Kameswari, Ganga, Uma, Chandi, Chamundi, Lalita, Gauri, Kundalini, Tara, Rajeswari, Tripurasundari, etc., are all Her forms. She is worshipped, during the nine days of the Dusserah as Durga, Lakshmi, and Saraswati. Devi is the Mother of all. The pious and the wicked, the rich and the poor, the saint and the sinner—all are Her children. Devi or Sakti is the Mother of Nature. She is Nature Itself. The whole world is Her body. Mountains are Her bones. Rivers are Her veins. Ocean is Her bladder. Sun, moon are Her eyes. Wind is Her breath. Agni is Her mouth. She runs this world show." —Swami Sivananda, *Devi*

Dharmakaya: (Sanskrit) Literally, "law body, or truth body." The ultimate nature of a fully awakened being. The Buddha Body of Reality. The highest of the bodies of a Buddha (see Kaya). The Dharmakaya is the archetypal "form" of an awakened being, that part which straddles the boundary between the unmanifested Absolute and manifested things. In Kabbalah, Dharmakaya corresponds to the sephirah Kether ("crown").

"Only those who possess the Dharmakaya body, the Law-body, the body which is Substance-Being, can enter into the temple of the Unmanifested Cosmic Mother... Those who enter into the bosom of the Great Reality possess the glorious body of Dharmakaya. Those who possess the body of Dharmakaya submerge themselves within the joy of life, free in its movement." —Samael Aun Weor, *The Gnostic Bible: The Pistis Sophia Unveiled*

Drukpa: (Also known variously as Druk-pa, Dugpa, Brugpa, Dag dugpa or Dad dugpa) The term Drukpa comes from from Dzongkha and Tibetan 'brug yul, which means "country of Bhutan," and is composed of Druk, "dragon," and pa, "person." In Asia, the word refers to the people of Bhutan, a country between India and Tibet.

Drukpa can also refer to a large sect of Buddhism which broke from the Kagyug-pa "the Ones of the Oral Tradition." They considered themselves as the heirs of the indian Gurus: their teaching, which goes back to Vajradhara, was conveyed through Dakini, from Naropa to Marpa and then to the ascetic and mystic poet Milarepa. Later on, Milarepa's disciples founded new monasteries, and new threads appeared, among which are the Karmapa and the Drukpa. All those schools form the Kagyug-pa order, in spite of episodic internal quarrels and extreme differences in practice. The Drukpa sect is recognized by their ceremonial large red hats, but it should be known that they are not the only "Red Hat" group (the Nyingmas, founded by Padmasambhava, also use red hats). The Drukpas have established a particular worship of the Dorje (Vajra, or thunderbolt, a symbol of the phallus).

Samael Aun Weor wrote repeatedly in many books that the "Drukpas" practice and teach Black Tantra, by means of the expelling of the sexual energy. If we analyze the word, it is clear that he is referring to "Black Dragons," or people who practice Black Tantra. He was not referring to all the people of Bhutan, or all members of the Buddhist Drukpa sect. Such a broad condemnation would be as ridiculous as the one made by all those who condemn all Jews for the crucifixion of Jesus.

"In 1387, with just reason, the Tibetan reformer Tsong Khapa cast every book of Necromancy that he found into flames. As a result, some discontent Lamas formed an alliance with the aboriginal Bhons, and today they form a powerful sect of black magic in the regions of Sikkim, Bhutan, and Nepal, submitting themselves to the most abominable black rites." —Samael Aun Weor, *The Revolution of Beelzebub*

Ego: The multiplicity of contradictory psychological elements that we have inside are in their sum the "ego." Each one is also called "an ego" or an "I." Every ego is a psychological defect which produces suffering. The ego is three (related to our Three Brains or three centers of psychological processing), seven (capital sins), and legion (in their infinite variations).

"The ego is the root of ignorance and pain." —Samael Aun Weor, *The Esoteric Treatise of Hermetic Astrology*

"The Being and the ego are incompatible. The Being and the ego are like water and oil. They can never be mixed... The annihilation of the psychic aggregates (egos) can be made possible only by radically comprehending our errors through meditation and by the evident Self-reflection of the Being." —Samael Aun Weor, *The Gnostic Bible: The Pistis Sophia Unveiled*

Elemental: the intelligence or soul of all creatures below the human kingdom, whose physical bodies are the minerals, plants and animals, but whose souls are gnomes, sprites, elves and fairies. (Strictly speaking, even intellectual animals remain as elementals until they create the soul; however in common usage the term elementals refers to the creatures of the three lower kingdoms: mineral, plant, and animal).

"In the times of King Arthur and the Knights of the Round Table, elementals of Nature were manifest everywhere, deeply penetrating our physical atmosphere. Many are the tales of elves, leprechauns and fairies, which still abound in green Erin, Ireland. Unfortunately, all these things of innocence, all this beauty from the soul of the Earth, is no longer perceived by humanity. This is due to the intellectual scoundrel's pedantries and the animal ego's excessive development." —Samael Aun Weor, *The Great Rebellion*

Ens Seminis: (Latin) Literally, "the entity of semen." A term used by Paracelsus.

Fornication: Originally, the term fornication was derived from the Indo-European word gwher, whose meanings relate to heat and burning. Fornication means to make the heat (solar fire) of the seed (sexual power) leave the body through voluntary orgasm. Any voluntary orgasm is fornication, whether between a married man and woman, or an unmarried man and woman, or through masturbation, or in any other case; this is explained by Moses: "A man from whom there is a discharge of semen, shall immerse all his flesh in water, and he shall remain unclean until evening. And any garment or any leather [object] which has semen on it, shall be immersed in water, and shall remain unclean until evening. A woman with whom a man cohabits, whereby there was [a discharge of] semen, they shall immerse in water, and they shall remain unclean until evening." —Leviticus 15:16-18

To fornicate is to spill the sexual energy through the orgasm. Those who "deny themselves" restrain the sexual energy, and "walk in the midst of the fire" without being burned. Those who restrain the sexual energy, who renounce the orgasm, remember God in themselves, and do not defile themselves with animal passion, "for the temple of God is holy, which temple ye are."

"Whosoever is born of God doth not commit sin; for his seed remaineth in him: and he cannot sin, because he is born of God." —1 John 3:9

This is why neophytes always took a vow of sexual abstention, so that they could prepare themselves for marriage, in which they would have sexual relations but not release the sexual energy through the orgasm. This is why Paul advised:

"...they that have wives be as though they had none..." —I Corinthians 7:29

"A fornicator is an individual who has intensely accustomed his genital organs to copulate (with orgasm). Yet, if the same individual changes his custom of copulation to the custom of no copulation, then he transforms himself into a chaste person. We have as an example the astonishing case of Mary Magdalene, who was a famous prostitute. Mary Magdalene became the famous Saint Mary Magdalene, the repented prostitute. Mary Magdalene became the chaste disciple of Christ." —Samael Aun Weor, *The Revolution of Beelzebub*

Gnosis: (Greek) Knowledge.

1. The word Gnosis refers to the knowledge we acquire through our own experience, as opposed to knowledge that we are told or believe in. Gnosis —by whatever name in history or culture —is conscious, experiential knowledge, not merely intellectual or conceptual knowledge, belief, or theory. This term is synonymous with the Hebrew "daath" and the Sanskrit "jna."

2. The tradition that embodies the core wisdom or knowledge of humanity.

"Gnosis is the flame from which all religions sprouted, because in its depth Gnosis is religion. The word "religion" comes from the Latin word "religare," which implies "to link the Soul to God"; so Gnosis is the very pure flame from where all religions sprout, because Gnosis is Knowledge, Gnosis is Wisdom." —Samael Aun Weor, The Esoteric Path

"The secret science of the Sufis and of the Whirling Dervishes is within Gnosis. The secret doctrine of Buddhism and of Taoism is within Gnosis. The sacred magic of the Nordics is within Gnosis. The wisdom of Hermes, Buddha, Confucius, Mohammed and Quetzalcoatl, etc., etc., is within Gnosis. Gnosis is the Doctrine of Christ." —Samael Aun Weor, *The Revolution of Beelzebub*

Heliogabalus Stone: A reference to the Cubic Stone of Yesod. Historically, a large black stone, a meteorite, that some describe from its image on coins and in sculpture as shaped like a bee-hive; others as phallic. This stone first appears in history atop its altar in the temple of Emesa on coins minted in the reign of Caracalla. It was taken by Varius Avitus Bassianus, Roman emperor (218-222), during his own reign, to Rome, and placed in a huge temple dedicated to it on the Palatine hill. Each summer, of the three he spent there, he led the stone in ceremonial procession, attended by musicians and dancers, to another palace in a garden at the outer edge of Rome. At the end of summer he would take it back to the Palatine. This is recorded in his coinage, as well as in the written sources. Varius was appointed priest of the sun-god Elagabal, whose name he adopted. Heliogabalus lived in Rome as an oriental despot and, giving himself up to detestable sensual pleasures, degraded the imperial office to the lowest point by most shameful vices, which had their origin in certain rites of oriental naturalistic religion.

Initiation: The process whereby the Innermost (the Inner Father) receives recognition, empowerment and greater responsibilities in the Internal Worlds, and little by little approaches His goal: complete Self-realization, or in other words, the return into the Absolute. Initiation NEVER applies to the "I" or our terrestrial personality.

"Nine Initiations of Minor Mysteries and seven great Initiations of Major Mysteries exist. The INNERMOST is the one who receives all of these Initiations. The Testament of Wisdom says: "Before the dawning of the false aurora upon the earth, the ones who survived the hurricane and the tempest were praising the INNERMOST, and the heralds of the aurora appeared unto them." The psychological "I" does not receives Initiations. The human personality does not receive anything. Nonetheless, the "I" of some Initiates becomes filled with pride when saying 'I am a Master, I have such Initiations.' Thus, this is how the "I" believes itself to be an Initiate and keeps reincarnating in order to "perfect itself", but, the "I" never ever perfects itself. The "I" only reincarnates in order to satisfy desires. That is all." —Samael Aun Weor, *The Aquarian Message*

Initiations of Major Mysteries: The qualifications of the consciousness as it ascends into greater degrees of wisdom. The first five Initiations of Major Mysteries correspond to the creation of the real Human Being. Learn more by studying these books by Samael Aun Weor: *The Perfect Matrimony, The Three Mountains,* and *The Revolution of Beelzebub.*

"High initiation is the fusion of two principles: Atman-Buddhi, through the five principal Initiations of Major Mysteries. With the first we achieve the fusion of Atman-Buddhi, and with the fifth, we add the Manas to this fusion, and so the septenary is reduced to a trinity: "Atman-Buddhi Manas." There are a total of Nine Initiations of Major Mysteries." —Samael Aun Weor, *The Zodiacal Course*

"We fulfill our human evolution with the five Initiations of Major Mysteries. The remaining three Initiations and the degree of "Lord of the World" are of a "Super-Human" nature." —Samael Aun Weor, *Esoteric Medicine and Practical Magic*

Initiations of Minor Mysteries: The probationary steps required of all who wish to enter into the path of Self-realization. These nine tests are given to all disciples who begin to perform the Gnostic work in themselves. Only those who complete these tests can receive the right to enter into the Major Mysteries. For more information, read *The Perfect Matrimony.*

"Remember that each one of the nine Initiations of Lesser Mysteries has a musical note and an instrument which produces it." —Samael Aun Weor, *The Revolution of Beelzebub*

"To want to rapidly become fused with the Innermost without having passed through the nine initiations of Lesser Mysteries is akin to wanting to receive a doctor's degree in medicine without having studied all the required years at university, or like wanting to be a general without having passed through all the military ranks." —Samael Aun Weor, *The Zodiacal Course*

"Throughout the Initiations of Lesser Mysteries, the disciple has to pass through the entire tragedy of Golgotha..." —Samael Aun Weor, *The Zodiacal Course*

Innermost: "Our real Being is of a universal nature. Our real Being is neither a kind of superior nor inferior "I." Our real Being is impersonal, universal, divine. He transcends every concept of "I," me, myself, ego, etc., etc." —Samael Aun Weor, The Perfect Matrimony

Also known as Atman, the Spirit, Chesed, our own individual interior divine Father.

"The Innermost is the ardent flame of Horeb. In accordance with Moses, the Innermost is the Ruach Elohim (the Spirit of God) who sowed the waters in the beginning of the world. He is the Sun King, our Divine Monad, the Alter-Ego of Cicerone." —Samael Aun Weor, *The Revolution of Beelzebub*

Internal Worlds: The many dimensions beyond the physical world. These dimensions are both subjective and objective. To know the objective internal worlds (the Astral Plane, or Nirvana, or the Klipoth) one must first know one's own personal, subjective internal worlds, because the two are intimately associated.

"Whosoever truly wants to know the internal worlds of the planet Earth or of the solar system or of the galaxy in which we live, must previously know his intimate world, his individual, internal life, his own internal worlds. Man, know thyself, and thou wilt know the Universe and its Gods. The more we explore this internal world called "myself," the more we will comprehend that we simultaneously live in two worlds, in two realities, in two confines: the external and the internal. In the same way that it is indispensable for one to learn how to walk in the external world so as not to fall down into a precipice, or not get lost in the streets of the city, or to select one's friends, or not associate with the perverse ones, or not eat poison, etc.; likewise, through the psychological work upon oneself we learn how to walk in the internal world, which is explorable only through Self-observation." —Samael Aun Weor, *Treatise of Revolutionary Psychology*

Through the work in Self-observation, we develop the capacity to awaken where previously we were asleep: including in the objective internal worlds.

Jinn State: The condition that results from moving the physical body into the fourth dimension. "A body while in the "Jinn" state can float in the air (Laghima) or be submerged within the waters (Prakamya), or pass through fire without being burned, or be reduced to the size of an atom (Anima), or be enlarged to the point of touching the sun or the moon with the hand (Mahima). A body submerged within the supra-sensible worlds is submitted to the laws of those worlds. Then, this body is plastic and elastic, so it can change form, decrease its weight (Laghima), or increase its weight (Garima) willingly... When Jesus was walking upon the waters of the Sea of Galilee, he had his body in the state of "Jinn." Peter was able to liberate himself from the chains and to leave the prison, thanks to the assistance of an Angel who helped him place his body in the state of "Jinn."" —Samael Aun Weor, *The Aquarian Message*

Kabbalah: (Hebrew) Alternatively spelled Cabala, Qabalah (etc., ad nauseam) from the Hebrew KBLH or QBL, "to receive." An ancient esoteric teaching hidden from the uninitiated, whose branches and many forms have reached throughout the world. The true Kabbalah is the science and language of the Superior Worlds and is thus Objective, complete and without flaw; it is said that "All Enlightened Beings Agree," and their natural agreement is a function of the Awakened Consciousness. The Kabbalah is the language of that Consciousness, thus disagreement regarding it's meaning and interpretation is always due to the Subjective elements in the psyche.

"The objective of studying the Kabbalah is to be skilled for work in the Internal Worlds... One that does not comprehend remains confused in the Internal Worlds. Kabbalah is the basis in order to understand the language of these worlds." —Samael Aun Weor, *Tarot and Kabbalah*

Kundalini: "Kundalini, the serpent power or mystic fire, is the primordial energy or Sakti that lies dormant or sleeping in the Muladhara Chakra, the centre of the body. It is called the serpentine or annular power on account of serpentine form. It is an electric fiery occult power, the great pristine force which underlies all organic and inorganic matter. Kundalini is the cosmic power in individual bodies. It is not a material force like electricity, magnetism, centripetal or centrifugal force. It is a spiritual potential Sakti or cosmic power. In reality it has no form. [...] O Divine Mother Kundalini, the Divine Cosmic Energy that is hidden in men! Thou art Kali, Durga, Adisakti, Rajarajeswari, Tripurasundari, Maha-Lakshmi, Maha-Sarasvati! Thou hast put on all these names and forms. Thou hast manifested as Prana, electricity, force, magnetism, cohesion, gravitation in this universe. This whole universe rests in Thy bosom. Crores of salutations unto thee. O Mother of this world! Lead me on to open the Sushumna Nadi and take Thee along the Chakras to Sahasrara Chakra and to merge myself in Thee and Thy consort, Lord Siva. Kundalini Yoga is that Yoga which treats of Kundalini Sakti, the six centres of spiritual energy (Shat Chakras), the arousing of the sleeping Kundalini Sakti and its union with Lord Siva in Sahasrara Chakra, at the crown of the head. This is an exact science. This is also known as Laya Yoga. The six centres are pierced (Chakra Bheda) by the passing of Kundalini Sakti to the top of the head. 'Kundala' means 'coiled'. Her form is like a coiled serpent. Hence the name Kundalini." — Swami Sivananda, *Kundalini Yoga*

Left-hand: In traditional cultures (especially Asian), the right hand is utilized for positive, clean, upright actions, such as eating, making offerings, etc., while the left hand is used for hidden, unclean, or harmful actions. This tradition emerged from the ancient esoteric knowledge, unknown to the public, in which the followers of the light (divinity, purity) correspond to the "right-hand of God" while the adherents of impurity and desire fall to the left, into disgrace. These contrary paths are rooted in Sanskrit terms. Dakshinachara (Sanskrit) literally means "upright in conduct" but is interpreted as "Right-Hand Path." Vamacara literally means "black magic," or "behaving badly or in the wrong way," and is used to refer to "Left-Hand Path" or "Left-path" (Sanskrit: Vamamarga). These two paths are explained in Kabbalah as well.

In modern times, those who follow the left-hand path have worked hard to make their path seem respectable and equal to the right, by claiming the two need each other to exist. This argument is based on the lie that left-hand initiates pursue the darkness of the Uncreated Light, the Absolute (which is pure, divine), yet the reality is that their degeneration and harmful acts propel them into the darkness of the abyss, the hell realms, to be cleansed of their impurity. Followers of the left-hand path believe they can outwit Divinity.

"And he shall separate them one from another, as a shepherd divideth his sheep from the goats. And he shall set the sheep on his right, but the goats on his left." —Matthew 25: 32-33

"Then the people of the right hand —Oh! how happy shall be the people of the right hand! And the people of the left hand —Oh! how wretched shall be the people of the left hand!" —Qur'an, Surah Al-Waqiah (The Inevitable) [56:8-9]

The widespread of the use of these terms in the West originated with H. P. Blavatsky.

It is important to note that physical handedness has nothing to do with one's spiritual level, value, or destiny. The persecution of left-handedness is just an ignorant form of discrimination.

"In symbolism the body is divided vertically into halves, the right half being considered as light and the left half as darkness. By those unacquainted with the true meanings of light and darkness the light half was denominated spiritual and the left half material. Light is the symbol of objectivity; darkness of subjectivity. Light is a manifestation of life and is therefore posterior to life. That which is anterior to light is darkness, in which light exists temporarily but darkness permanently. As life precedes light, its only symbol is darkness, and darkness is considered as the veil which must eternally conceal the true nature of abstract and undifferentiated Being.

"In ancient times men fought with their right arms and defended the vital centers with their left arms, on which was carried the protecting shield. The right half of the body was regarded therefore as offensive and the left half defensive. For this reason also the right side of the body was considered masculine and the left side feminine. Several authorities are of the opinion that the present prevalent right-handedness of the race is the outgrowth of the custom of holding the left hand in restraint for defensive purposes. Furthermore, as the source of Being is in the primal darkness which preceded light, so the spiritual nature of man is in the dark part of his being, for the heart is on the left side.

"Among the curious misconceptions arising from the false practice of associating darkness with evil is one by which several early nations used the right hand for all constructive labors and the left hand for only those purposes termed unclean and unfit for the sight of the gods. For the same reason black magic was often referred to as the left-hand path, and heaven was said to be upon the right and hell upon the left. Some philosophers further declared that there were two methods of writing: one from left to right, which was considered the exoteric method; the other from right to left, which was considered esoteric. The exoteric writing was that which was done out or away from the heart, while the esoteric writing was that which--like the ancient Hebrew--was written toward the heart." —Manly P. Hall, *The Secret Teachings of All Ages*

Lilith: (also Lilit; Hebrew לילית, "the night visitor") An ancient symbol appearing in Sumerian mythology (4000 BC). In the Zohar she is described as the feminine half or the first "wife" of Adam (the first man), and is the origin of many demonic spirits (elementaries) who plague mankind, including the sucubi and incubi generated by masturbation and sexual fantasy.

"In a hole by the great, supernal abyss, there is a certain female, a spirit above all spirits. We have explained that its name is Lilit. She was first with Adam, being his wife... In ancient books, it has been said that Lilit fled from Adam before that, namely before Eve was prepared. We did not understand it this way, because this female, Lilit, was with him. As long as this woman, Eve, was not made to be with Adam, Lilit was with him. When Eve was designed to be with him, Lilit fled to the sea, destined to harm the world." —Zohar

"...Lilith, the great mother of the demons..." —Zohar

"Lilith is the mother of abortions, homosexuality, and in general, all kinds of crimes against Nature." —Samael Aun Weor, *The Perfect Matrimony*

"Kabbalistic traditions tell us that Adam had two wives: Lilith and Nahemah. It is stated that Lilith is the mother of abortion, homosexuality, mother of sexual degeneration, and Nahemah is the mother of adultery, fornication, etc. Lilith and Nahemah are the two aspects of infrasexuality. These two women cor- respond to two submerged spheres within the very interior of the Earth, the infradimensional and the mineral." —Samael Aun Weor, *Tarot and Kabbalah*

Also:

"Another small moon called Lilith by astronomers also exists. Lilith is the black moon. The souls that have already totally separated themselves from their Monad formed by Atman-Buddhi-Manas, go there." —Samael Aun Weor, *The Zodiacal Course*

Logos: (Greek) means Verb or Word. In Greek and Hebrew metaphysics, the unifying principle of the world. The Logos is the manifested deity of every nation and people; the outward expression or the effect of the cause which is ever concealed. (Speech is the "logos" of thought). The Logos has three aspects, known universally as the Trinity or Trimurti. The First Logos is the Father, Brahma. The Second Logos is the Son, Vishnu. The Third Logos is the Holy Spirit, Shiva. One who incarnates the Logos becomes a Logos.

"The Logos is not an individual. The Logos is an army of ineffable beings." —Samael Aun Weor, *Sexology, the Basis of Endocrinology and Criminology*

Lord's Prayer:

Our Father, Who art in heaven,
Hallowed be Thy Name.
Thy Kingdom come.
Thy Will be done, on earth as it is in Heaven.
Give us this day our daily bread.
And forgive us our trespasses, as we forgive those who trespass against us.
And lead us not into temptation, but deliver us from evil. Amen.

Lumisial: "A place of light." A Gnostic Lumisial is a generator of spiritual energy, a Gnostic school which maintains the ancient initiatic Three Chamber structure. The source of power is the Cosmic Christ, and the means to receive and transform it are within the Second and Third Chambers.

"We are therefore working, my dear brethren, to initiate the Era of Aquarius. We are working in order to save what is possible, meaning, those who allow themselves to be saved. This is why it is necessary that we shape our Gnostic Movements and that we organize them each time better; that we establish the Three Chambers. Our Gnostic Movements must have exactly Three Chambers. Each Lumisial must have Three Chambers for the instruction of our students. Our Gnostic Centers receive a name in a very pure language that flows like a river of gold that runs in the sunny, thick jungle; that name is LUMISIALS." —Samael Aun Weor, The Final Catastrophe and the Extraterrestrials

Lunar: From Latin lunaris "of the moon," from luna luna, the Moon. The Romans called the moon goddess Luna, which in Greek is Selene.

In esotericism, the term lunar is generally used in concert with its solar companion, and this duality can have many implications. In Western esotericism and the writings of Samael Aun Weor, the lunar aspect is seen as feminine, cold, and polarized as negative (not "bad," just the opposite polarity of solar, which is positive). In Asian mysticism, the symbolic genders are often reversed, with the lunar current seen as masculine and related to Chandra, the masculine moon god.

Some example uses of the term lunar:

1. In general "lunar" can indicate something that proceeds mechanically, automatically, — like the movements of the Moon, tides, seasons, etc. — according to the fundamental natural laws. While this is perfectly normal, it is inferior to the solar attributes, which are not bound by mechanical movements, but instead have liberty, freedom of movement, etc.

2. In another context, for example within the body, there are lunar and solar currents. Within us, the lunar current is fallen into disgrace and must be restored, while the solar current remains intact.

3. There are solar and lunar religions: a lunar religion faces backwards, looking only at the past, and remains attached to traditions, habits, mechanical rules. A lunar mind is similar.

4. The lunar bodies are the vehicles we receive from nature automatically: the physical body, vital body, and astral-mental body. Since they were made by nature, they must be returned to nature, thus they are not immortal, eternal, thereby illustrating the need to create solar bodies, which transcend the mechanical, lunar laws of nature.

Magic: The word magic is derived from the ancient word "mag" that means priest. Real magic is the work of a priest. A real magician is a priest.

"Magic, according to Novalis, is the art of influencing the inner world consciously." —Samael Aun Weor, *The Mystery of the Golden Flower*

"When magic is explained as it really is, it seems to make no sense to fanatical people. They prefer to follow their world of illusions." —Samael Aun Weor, *The Revolution of Beelzebub*

Mantra: (Sanskrit, literally "mind protection") A sacred word or sound. The use of sacred words and sounds is universal throughout all religions and mystical traditions, because the root of all creation is in the Great Breath or the Word, the Logos. "In the beginning was the Word..."

Master: Like many terms related to spirituality, this one is grossly misunderstood. Samael Aun Weor wrote while describing the Germanic Edda, "In this Genesis of creation we discover Sexual Alchemy. The Fire fecundated the cold waters of chaos. The masculine principle Alfadur fecundated the feminine principle Niffleheim, dominated by Surtur (the Darkness), to bring forth life. That is how Ymir is born, the father of the giants, the Internal God of every human being, the Master." Therefore, the Master is the Innermost, Atman, the Father.

"The only one who is truly great is the Spirit, the Innermost. We, the intellectual animals, are leaves that the wind tosses about... No student of occultism is a Master. True Masters are only those who have reached the Fifth Initiation of Major Mysteries. Before the Fifth Initiation nobody is a Master." —Samael Aun Weor, *The Perfect Matrimony*

Maya: (Sanskrit, literally "appearance, illusion, deception") Can indicate 1) the illusory nature of existence, 2) the womb of the Divine Mother, or 3) the Divine Mother Herself.

Meditation: "When the esoterist submerges himself into meditation, what he seeks is information." —Samael Aun Weor

"It is urgent to know how to meditate in order to comprehend any psychic aggregate, or in other words, any psychological defect. It is indispensable to know how to work with all our heart and with all our soul, if we want the elimination to occur." —Samael Aun Weor, *The Gnostic Bible: The Pistis Sophia Unveiled*

"1. The Gnostic must first attain the ability to stop the course of his thoughts, the capacity to not think. Indeed, only the one who achieves that capacity will hear the Voice of the Silence.

"2. When the Gnostic disciple attains the capacity to not think, then he must learn to concentrate his thoughts on only one thing.

"3. The third step is correct meditation. This brings the first flashes of the new consciousness into the mind.

"4. The fourth step is contemplation, ecstasy or Samadhi. This is the state of Turiya (perfect clairvoyance). —Samael Aun Weor, *The Perfect Matrimony*

Melchisedec: (Hebrew מלכי־צדק. Alternatively, Malkhi-tzedek, Malki Tzedek, or Melchisedek, which means "king of justice / virtue") See Gen. 14:18-20, Ps. 110:4, and Epistle to the Hebrews, ch. 7.

"Malkhi-tzedek king of Salem brought forth bread and wine. He was a priest to God, the Most High. He blessed [Abram], and said, 'Blessed be Abram to God Most High, Possessor of heaven and earth. And blessed be God Most High, who delivered your enemies into your hand.' [Abram then] gave him a tenth of everything." —Genesis / Bereshit 14:18-20

"[Jesus] Who in the days of his flesh, when he had offered up prayers and supplications with strong crying and tears unto him that was able to save him from death, and was heard in that he feared; Though he were a Son, yet learned he obedience by the things which he suffered; And being made perfect, he became the author of eternal salvation unto all them that obey him; Called of God an high priest after the order of Melchisedec. Of whom we have many things to say, and hard to be uttered, seeing ye are dull of hearing." —Hebrews 5

"And Melchisedec, the Receiver of the Light; purifieth those powers and carrieth their light into the Treasury of the Light, while the servitors of all the rulers gather together all matter from them all; and the servitors of all the rulers of the Fate and the servitors of the sphere which is below the æons, take it and fashion it into souls of men and cattle and reptiles and wild-beasts and birds, and send them down into the world of mankind." —*The Pistis Sophia*

"Melchisedec is the planetary Genie of the Earth, of whom Jesus, the great Kabir, gave testimony. Melchisedec is the Great Receiver of the Cosmic Light. Melchisedec has a physical body. He is a Man, or better if we say, he is a Super-Man. The Kingdom of Agharti is found in the subterranean caverns of the Earth. The Earth is hollow and the network of caverns constitute Agharti. The Genie of the Earth lives in Agharti with a group of survivors from Lemuria and Atlantis. The Goros, powerful Lords of life and death, work with Melchisedec. The whole ancient wisdom of the centuries has been recorded on Stone, within the Kingdom of Agharti." — Samael Aun Weor, *The Gnostic Bible: The Pistis Sophia Unveiled*

"If Jesus was God incarnate, as the solemn councils of the church discovered, why is He referred to in the New Testament as "called of God an high prim after the order of Melchizedek"? The words "after the order" make Jesus one of a line or order of which there must have been others of equal or even superior dignity. If the "Melchizedeks" were the divine or priestly rulers of the nations of the earth before the inauguration of the system of temporal rulers, then the statements attributed to St. Paul would indicate that Jesus either was one of these "philosophic elect" or was attempting to reestablish their system of government. It will be remembered that Melchizedek also performed the same ceremony of the drinking of wine and the breaking of bread as did Jesus at the Last Supper." —Manly P. Hall, *The Secret Teachings of All Ages*

Mithras: Zoroastrian symbol of Christ.

"The Hindus called the Sun SURYA; the Persians, MITHRAS; the Egyptians, OSIRIS; the Assyrians and Chaldæans, BEL; the Scythians and Etruscans and the ancient Pelasgi, ARKALEUS or HERCULES; the Phœnicians, ADONAI or ADON; and the Scandinavians, ODIN...

"MITHRAS was the Sun-God of the Persians; and was fabled to have been born in a grotto or cave, at the Winter Solstice. His feasts were celebrated at that period, at the moment when the sun commenced to return Northward, and to increase the length of the days. This was the great Feast of the Magian religion. The Roman Calendar, published in the time of Constantine, at which period his worship began to gain ground in the Occident, fixed his feast-day on the 25th of December. His statues and images were inscribed, Deo-Soli invicto Mithræ--to the invincible Sun-God Mithras. Nomen invictum Sol Mithra. . . . Soli Omnipotenti Mithræ. To him, gold, incense, and myrrh were consecrated. "Thee," says Martianus Capella, in his hymn to the Sun, "the dwellers on the Nile adore as Serapis, and Memphis worships as Osiris; in the sacred rites of Persia thou art Mithras, in Phrygia, Atys, and Libya bows down to thee as Ammon, and Phœnician Byblos as Adonis; and thus the whole world adores thee under different names." [...]

"Mithras, the rock-born hero, heralded the Sun's return in Spring, as Prometheus, chained in his cavern, betokened the continuance of Winter. The Persian beacon on the mountain-top represented the Rock-born Divinity enshrined in his worthiest temple; and the funeral conflagration of Hercules was the sun dying in glory behind the Western hills. But though the transitory manifestation suffers or dies, the abiding and eternal power liberates and saves. It was an essential attribute of a Titan, that he should arise again after his fall; for the revival of Nature is as certain as its decline, and its alternations are subject to the appointment of a power which controls them both...

"Mithras is not only light, but intelligence; that luminary which, though born in obscurity, will not only dispel darkness but conquer death...

"Between life and death, between sunshine and shade, Mithras is the present exemplification of the Primal Unity from which all things arose, and into which, through his mediation, all contrarieties will ultimately be absorbed. His annual sacrifice is the Passover of the Magi, a symbolical atonement or pledge of moral and physical regeneration. He created the world in the beginning; and as at the close of each successive year he sets free the current of life to invigorate a fresh circle of being, so in the end of all things he will bring the weary sum of ages as a hecatomb before God, releasing by a final sacrifice the Soul of Nature from her perishable frame, to commence a brighter and purer existence." —Albert Pike (1871)

"The TAU cross was inscribed on the forehead of every person admitted into the Mysteries of Mithras... Concerning the crucifixion of the Persian Mithras, J. P. Lundy has written: "Dupuis tells us that Mithra was put to death by crucifixion, and rose again on the 25th of March. In the Persian Mysteries the body of a young man, apparently dead, was exhibited, which was feigned to be restored to life. By his sufferings he was believed to have worked their salvation, and on this account he was called their Savior. His priests watched his tomb to the midnight of the vigil of the 25th of March, with loud cries, and in darkness; when all at once the light burst forth from all parts, the priest cried, Rejoice, O sacred initiated, your God is risen. His death, his pains, and sufferings, have worked your salvation." —Manly P. Hall, *The Secret Teachings of All Ages*

Nahemah: Or Naamah. (Hebrew נעמה) A symbol in Kabbalah related to lust, seduction, and the infernal worlds (Klipoth, hell).

"...she also bare Tubalcain, an instructor of every artificer in brass and iron: and the sister of Tubalcain [was] Naamah [נעמה]." —Genesis 4:22

"And Rehoboam the son of Solomon reigned in Judah. Rehoboam [was] forty and one years old when he began to reign, and he reigned seventeen years in Jerusalem, the city which the LORD did choose out of all the tribes of Israel, to put his name there. And his mother's name [was] Naamah an Ammonitess. And Judah did evil in the sight of the LORD, and they provoked him to jealousy with their sins which they had committed, above all that their fathers had done." —1 Kings 14

"Rabbi Chiya quotes, "And the sister of Tuval Kayin was Naamah" (Beresheet 4:22). Why do the scriptures mention her name, Naamah (tender)? It is because people were seduced by her, and spirits and demons. Rabbi Yitzchak said that the sons of Elohim, Aza, and Azael were seduced by her. [...] Adam had intercourse with the female spirits for 130 years until Naamah came. Because of her beauty, she led the sons of Elohim, Aza and Azael astray. She bore them. Evil spirits and demons spread out from her into the world. They wander around the world during the night, deriding human beings and causing nocturnal pollution. Wherever they find men sleeping alone in their own homes, they hover over them and cling to them, arousing lustful desires and having offspring by them." —The Zohar

"Nahemah is the mother of malignant beauty, passion and adultery." — Samael Aun Weor, *The Perfect Matrimony*

Another interesting appearance of this name is in Genesis 3:

"And when the woman saw that the tree [was] good for food, and that it [was] pleasant to the eyes, and a tree נחמד [to be desired] to make [one] wise, she took of the fruit thereof, and did eat, and gave also unto her husband with her; and he did eat." —Genesis 3

Philosophical Stone: An Alchemical symbol of the Intimate Christ dressed with bodies of Gold. When acquired, this stone gives powers over nature. It is lost when thrown in water (through fornication). When the stone is dissolved in (sexual) water, then the metallic Spirit is melted, and interior Magnes escapes. It is said when this happens, one dissolves the stone in water on Saturday (Saturn = death). The Philosophical Stone is passes through phases of development: black, red & white. It is also the Cubic stone of Yesod (Parsifal Unveiled), the stone that Jacob anointed with oil and "a Stone of stumbling, a rock of offense."

Nicolas Valois: "It is a Stone of great virtue, and is called a Stone and is not a stone."

Pratyeka Buddha: Sanskrit प्रत्येकबुद्ध. Pratyeka is from Sanskrit, prati, meaning "towards, for"; eka, the numeral "one", thus meaning "for oneself," or "selfish." Buddha means "awakened." Thus, the term pratyeka buddha refers to someone who awakens consciousness by themselves, for themselves, as opposed to doing so out of compassion for others.

"We must make a complete differentiation between the Sravakas and Pratyeka Buddhas on one side, and Bodhisattvas on the other. The Sravakas and Pratyeka-Buddhas preoccupy themselves only with their particular perfection, without caring a bit for this poor suffering humanity. Obviously, the Pratyeka Buddhas and Sravakas can never incarnate Christ. Only the Bodhisattvas who sacrifice themselves for humanity can incarnate Christ. The sacred title of Bodhisattva is legitimately attained only by those who have renounced all Nirvanic happiness for the love of this suffering humanity." —Samael Aun Weor, *The Gnostic Bible: The Pistis Sophia Unveiled*

Resurrected Master: A master who has completed the Second Mountain (thereby eliminating the entirety of their defects), has died physically, and has resurrected in a new physical body. The story of Jesus of Nazareth provides a clear example. After resurrection the master enters the Third Mountain, the Mountain of Ascension. This type of master has no ego (pride, lust, anger, etc), but still needs to work a lot in order to gain the right to enter into the Absolute.

"Every resurrected master has solar bodies, but does not have lunar bodies. The resurrected masters have powers over fire, air, water and the earth. Resurrected masters can transmute physical lead into physical gold. The resurrected masters govern life and death. They can conserve the physical body for millions of years. They know the quadrature of the circle and the perpetual movement. They have the universal medicine, and speak the very pure language of the divine tongue which, like a golden river, flows delightfully through the thick, sunny jungle." —Samael Aun Weor, *The Esoteric Treatise of Hermetic Astrology*

"The [number of] resurrected masters can be counted on the fingers of the hands. [...] Hermes, Cagliostro, Paracelsus, Nicholas Flamel, Quetzalcoatl, St. Germain, Babaji, etc., preserved their physical bodies for thousands, and even millions of years, without death harming them. They are resurrected masters." —Samael Aun Weor, *Alchemy and Kabbalah in the Tarot*

"Indeed, there is no resurrection without death, nor a dawn within nature (or within the human being) without darkness, sorrows, and nocturnal agony preceding them, which makes their light more adorable." —Samael Aun Weor, *The Three Mountains*

"After the resurrection, the master does not die again. He is eternal. With this immortal body, he can appear and disappear instantaneously. Masters can make themselves visible in the physical world at will.

"Jesus the Christ is a Resurrected Master who for three days had his physical body in the Holy sepulcher. After the resurrection, Jesus appeared before the disciples who were on their way to the village of Emmaus and dined with them. After this, he was before the unbelieving Thomas, who only believed when he put his fingers in the wounds of the holy body of the great master.

"Hermes, Cagliostro, Paracelsus, Nicholas Flamel, Quetzalcoatl, St. Germain, Babaji, etc. preserved their physical body thousands and even millions of years ago without death harming them. They are resurrected masters." —Samael Aun Weor, *Tarot and Kabbalah*

"All the masters who have resurrected live with their physical bodies for millions of years... Only the initiates who have reached these summits can live and direct the current of life of the centuries. Only here the initiate no longer needs a spouse. The initiate's physical body remains in Jinn state; this is the gift of Cupid. Nevertheless, the initiate can become visible and tangible in this tridimensional world wherever is necessary, and works in the physical world under the commands of the White Lodge. As a Resurrected Master, the initiate commands the great life; he has power over the fire, air, water, and earth. Yes, all of Nature kneels before him and obeys him. He can live among men, and becomes a human-god.

"Naturally, it is indispensable to undergo the ordeals of the Arcanum Thirteen in order to reach these summits (Second Mountain). The physical body must be embalmed for death. The supper at Bethany corresponds to this event of the Arcanum Thirteen. Thus, after the body has been embalmed for death, it is submitted to a special evolution for the tomb that develops within the numbers thirty and thirty-five, which when added together give the Arcanum Eleven (the tamed lion); yes, we have to tame nature and overcome it.

"Thus, when the body is ready for the sepulcher, the processes of death and resurrection occur. In this case, the Angels of Death do not cut the silver cord; this is how the initiate dies but does not die. The physical brain of the initiate is submitted to a special transformation: it becomes more subtle, delicate, and radiant.

"The supper at Bethany relates with these processes of Jesus Christ.

"Now when Jesus was in Bethany, in the house of Simon the leper, There came unto him a woman having an alabaster jar of very precious ointment, and poured it on his head, as he sat at meat. But when his disciples saw it, they had indignation, saying, To what purpose is this waste? For this ointment might have been sold for much, and given to the poor. When Jesus understood it, he said unto them, Why trouble ye the woman? for she hath wrought a good work upon me. For ye have the poor always with you; but me ye have not always; for in that she hath poured this ointment on my body, she did it for my burial. Verily I say unto you, wherever this gospel shall be preached in the whole world, there shall also this, that this woman hath done, be told for a memorial of her." —Matthew, 26: 6-13 —Samael Aun Weor, *The Major Mysteries*

Samadhi: (Sanskrit) Literally means "union" or "combination" and its Tibetan equivilent means "adhering to that which is profound and definitive," or ting nge dzin, meaning "To hold unwaveringly, so there is no movement." Related terms include satori, ecstasy, manteia, etc. Samadhi is a state of consciousness. In the west, the term is used to describe an ecstatic state of consciousness in which the Essence escapes the painful limitations of the mind (the "I") and therefore experiences what is real: the Being, the Great Reality. There are many levels of Samadhi. In the sutras and tantras the term Samadhi has a much broader application whose precise interpretation depends upon which school and teaching is using it.

"Ecstasy is not a nebulous state, but a transcendental state of wonderment, which is associated with perfect mental clarity." —Samael Aun Weor, *The Elimination of Satan's Tail*

Satan: (Hebrew, opposer, or adversary) (Hebrew שטן, opposer, or adversary)

"And שטן [Satan] stood up against Israel..." —1 Chronicles 21:1

Although modern Christians have made Satan into a cartoon character, the reality is very different.

Within us, Satan is the fallen Lucifer, who is born within the psyche of every human being by means of the sexual impulse that culminates in the orgasm or sexual spasm of the fornicators. Satan, the fallen Lucifer, directs the lustful animal currents towards the atomic infernos of the human being, thus it becomes the profoundly evil adversary of our Innermost (God) and human values within our own psyche. This is why it is often identified with the leader of the fallen angels or fallen human values (parts) of our consciousness trapped within the animal mind (legions of egos, defects, vices of the mind) in other words, Satan is the Devil or "evil" adversary of God that everybody carries within their own psychological interior. The spiritual aspirant has to conquer Satan and transform him back into Lucifer, which is Latin for "bearer of Light." This was once known in

Christianity (even some popes were named Lucifer), but over the centuries Christianity degenerated.

"The white magician worships the inner Christ. The black magician worships Satan. This is the "I," the me, myself, the reincarnating ego. In fact, the "I" is the specter of the threshold itself. It continually reincarnates to satisfy desires. The "I" is memory. In the "I" are all of the memories of our ancient personalities. The "I" is Ahriman, Lucifer, Satan. Our real Being is the inner Christ. Our real Being is of a universal nature. Our real Being is not a superior or inferior "I." Our real Being is impersonal, universal, divine. He transcends every concept of "I," me, myself, ego, etc. The black magician strengthens his Satan and upon this he bases his fatal power. Satan's form and size result from the degree of human evil. When we enter the path of the perfect marriage, Satan loses his volume and ugliness. We need to dissolve Satan." —Samael Aun Weor, *The Perfect Matrimony*

"The origin of the sinful "I" lies in lust. The ego, Satan, is subject to the law of the eternal return of all things. It returns to new wombs in order to satisfy desires. In each one of its lives, the "I" repeats the same dramas, the same errors. The "I" complicates itself over time, each time becoming more and more perverse. The Satan that we carry within is composed of atoms of the Secret Enemy. Satan had a beginning; Satan has an end. We need to dissolve Satan in order to return to the inner star that has always smiled upon us. This is true final liberation. Only by dissolving the "I" can we attain absolute liberation." —Samael Aun Weor, *The Perfect Matrimony*

"Pain cannot make anyone perfect. If pain could perfect anyone, then all humanity would already be perfect. Pain is a result of our own errors. Satan commits many errors. Satan reaps the fruits of his errors. This fruit is pain. Therefore, pain is satanic. Satan cannot perfect himself, nor can he make anyone perfect. Pain cannot make anything perfect, because pain is of Satan. The great divine reality is happiness, peace, abundance, and perfection. The great reality cannot create pain. What is perfect cannot create pain. What is perfect can only engender happiness. Pain was created by the "I" (Satan)." —Samael Aun Weor, *The Perfect Matrimony*

"Time is Satan; Satan is memory. Satan is a bunch of memories. When a human being dies, only his memories remain. These memories constitute the "I," the me, myself, the reincarnating ego. Those unsatisfied desires, those memories of yesterday, reincarnate. Thus, this is how we are slaves of the past. Therefore, we can be sure that the past is what conditions our present life. We can affirm that Satan is time. We can also state, without fear of being mistaken, that time cannot liberate us from this valley of tears because time is Satanic. We have to learn to live from moment to moment. Life is an eternal now, an eternal present. Satan was the creator of time; those who think they will liberate themselves in a distant future, within some millions of years, with the passing of time and the ages, are sure candidates for the Abyss and the Second Death, because time is of Satan. Time does not liberate anyone. Satan enslaves; Satan does not liberate. We need to liberate ourselves right now. We need to live from moment to moment." —Samael Aun Weor, *The Perfect Matrimony*

Second Death: The complete dissolution of the ego in the infernal regions of nature, which in the end (after unimaginable quantities of suffering) purifies the Essence of all sin (karma) so that it may try again to reach complete development.

"He that overcometh (the sexual passion) shall inherit all things; and I will be his God (I will incarnate myself within him), and he shall be my son (because he is a Christified one), But the fearful (the tenebrous, cowards, unbelievers), and unbelieving, and the abominable, and murderers, and whoremongers, and sorcerers, and idolaters, and all liars, shall have their part in the lake which burneth with fire and brimstone: which is the second death. (Revelation 21) This lake which burns with fire and brimstone is the lake of carnal passion. This lake is related with the lower animal depths of the human being and its atomic region is the abyss. The tenebrous slowly disintegrate themselves within the abyss until they die. This is the second death." —Samael Aun Weor, *The Aquarian Message*

Secret Enemy: "The Nous atom is sometimes called by the occultist the white or good principle of the heart. We will now speak of its opposite: the dark atom or Secret Enemy. In many ways its activities are similar to the Nous atom; for it has legions of atomic entities under its command; but they are destructive and not constructive. This Secret Enemy resides in the lower section of the spine, and its atoms oppose the student's attempts to unite himself to his Innermost. The Secret Enemy has so much power in the atmosphere of this world that they can limit our thoughts and imprison our minds... The Secret Enemy works in every way to deny us any intelligence that would illuminate our minds, and would seek to stamp man into a machine cursed with similarity and a mind lacking all creative power... Man easily degenerates when in the power of the Secret Enemy; it preys upon the burning furnace of his desires, and when he weakens he is lost and sometimes cannot regain contact with his Innermost for two or three lives wherein he works out the karma of his evil desires." —M, *The Dayspring of Youth*

Self-observation: An exercise of attention, in which one learns to become an indifferent observer of one's own psychological process. True Self-observation is an active work of directed attention, without the interference of thought.

"We need attention intentionally directed towards the interior of our own selves. This is not a passive attention. Indeed, dynamic attention proceeds from the side of the observer, while thoughts and emotions belong to the side which is observed." —Samael Aun Weor, *Treatise of Revolutionary Psychology*

Self-realization: The achievement of perfect knowledge. This phrase is better stated as, "The realization of the Innermost Self," or "The realization of the true nature of self." At the ultimate level, this is the experiential, conscious knowledge of the Absolute, which is synonymous with Emptiness, Shunyata, or Non-being.

Self-remembering: A state of active consciousness, controlled by will, that begins with awareness of being here and now. This state has many levels (see: Consciousness). True Self-remembering occurs without thought or mental processing: it is a state of conscious perception and includes the remembrance of the inner Being.

Semen: The sexual energy of any creature or entity. In Gnosis, "semen" is a term used for the sexual energy of both masculine and feminine bodies. English semen originally meant 'seed of male animals' in the 14th century, and it was not applied to human males until the 18th century. It came from Latin semen, "seed of plants," from serere `to sow.' The Latin goes back to the Indo-European root *se-, source of seed, disseminate, season, seminar, and seminal. The word seminary (used for religious schools) is derived from semen and originally meant 'seedbed.'

That the semen is the source of all virtue is known from the word "seminal," derived from the Latin "semen," and which is defined as "highly original and influencing the development of future events: a seminal artist; seminal ideas."

In the esoteric tradition of pure sexuality, the word semen refers to the sexual energy of the organism, whether male or female. This is because male and female both carry the "seed" within: in order to create, the two "seeds" must be combined.

Sephirah: (Hebrew) plural: Sephiroth. literally, "jewel."

1. An emanation of Deity.

"The Ten Sephiroth of universal vibration emerge from the Ain Soph, which is the Microcosmic Star that guides our interior. This Star is the Real Being of our Being. Ten Sephiroth are spoken of, but in reality there are Twelve; the Ain Soph is the eleventh, and its tenebrous antithesis is in the Abyss, which is the twelfth Sephirah. These are twelve spheres or universal regions which mutually penetrate and co-penetrate without confusion." —Samael Aun Weor, *Tarot and Kabbalah*

2. A name of the Divine Mother.

Sexual Magic: The word magic is dervied from the ancient word magos "one of the members of the learned and priestly class," from O.Pers. magush, possibly from PIE *magh- "to be able, to have power." [Quoted from On-line Etymology Dictionary].

"All of us possess some electrical and magnetic forces within, and, just like a magnet, we exert a force of attraction and repulsion... Between lovers that magnetic force is particularly powerful and its action has a far-reaching effect. —Samael Aun Weor, *The Mystery of the Golden Flower*

Sexual magic refers to an ancient science that has been known and protected by the purest, most spiritually advanced human beings, whose purpose and goal is the harnessing and perfection of our sexual forces. A more accurate translation of sexual magic would be "sexual priesthood."

In ancient times, the priest was always accompanied by a priestess, for they represent the divine forces at the base of all creation: the masculine and feminine, the Yab-Yum, Ying-Yang, Father-Mother: the Elohim.

Unfortunately, the term "sexual magic" has been grossly misinterpreted by mistaken persons such as Aleister Crowley, who advocated a host of degenerated practices, all of which belong solely to the lowest and most perverse mentality. This website and the teachings presented here reject all such philosophies, theories, and practices, for they lead only to the enslavement of the consciousness, the worship of lust and desire, and the decay of humanity.

True, upright, heavenly sexual magic is the natural harnessing of our latent forces, making them active and harmonious with nature and the divine.

"People are filled with horror when they hear about sexual magic; however, they are not filled with horror when they give themselves to all kinds of sexual perversion and to all kinds of carnal passion." —Samael Aun Weor, *The Perfect Matrimony*

Solar: From Latin solaris "of the sun," from luna sol, the Sun. The Romans called the sun god Sol, which in Greek is Helios.

In esotericism, the term solar is generally used in concert with its lunar companion, and this duality can have many implications. In Western esotericism and the writings of Samael Aun Weor, the solar aspect is seen as masculine, warm, and polarized as positive (+), not "good," just the opposite polarity of lunar, which is negative (-).

In Asian mysticism, the solar current is related to Surya, the Sun god.

In esotericism of all types, the solar influence is related to the Absolute Sun, also called Christ, Avalokitesvara, Vishnu, Amitabha, etc. That is why all religions have solar deities, or "sun gods."

Some example uses of the term solar:

1. In general "solar" can indicate something that proceeds consciously guided by conscious acts, as opposed to the automatic, mechanical, lunar processes of nature.

2. In another context, for example within the body, there are lunar and solar currents. Within us, the lunar current is fallen into disgrace and must be restored, while the solar current remains intact.

3. There are solar and lunar religions: a lunar religion faces backwards, looking only at the past, and remains attached to traditions, habits, mechanical rules. A lunar mind is similar. A solar religion is concerned with the present, and lets go of the past.

4. The lunar bodies are the vehicles we receive from nature automatically: the physical body, vital body, and astral-mental body. Since they were made by nature, they must be returned to nature, thus they are not immortal,

eternal, thereby illustrating the need to create solar bodies, which transcend the mechanical, lunar laws of nature. Solar bodies are not made by mechanical lunar nature, but by a special, conscious process hidden in all religions but known only to a few.

Solar Bodies: The physical, vital, astral, mental, and casual bodies that are created through the beginning stages of Alchemy/Tantra and that provide a basis for existence in their corresponding levels of nature, just as the physical body does in the physical world. These bodies or vehicles are superior due to being created out of solar (Christic) energy, as opposed to the inferior, lunar bodies we receive from nature. Also known as the Wedding Garment (Christianity), the Merkabah (Kabbalah), To Soma Heliakon (Greek), and Sahu (Egyptian).

"All the masters of the White Lodge, the Angels, Archangels, Thrones, Seraphim, Virtues, etc., etc., etc. are garbed with the solar bodies. Only those who have solar bodies have the Being incarnated. Only someone who possesses the Being is an authentic Human Being." —Samael Aun Weor, The Esoteric Treatise of Hermetic Astrology

Son of Man: "When the Beloved One [Christ] becomes transformed into the soul , and when the soul becomes transformed into the Beloved One, that which we call the Son of Man is born from this ineffable, divine, and human mixture. The great Lord of Light, being the Son of the living God, becomes the Son of Man when he transform himself into the Human Soul. The Sun-Man is the result of all our purifications and bitterness. The Sun-Man is divine and human. The Son of Man is the final outcome of the human being. He is the child of our sufferings, the solemn mystery of the transubstantiation." —Samael Aun Weor, The Aquarian Message

"The Son of Man is born in the Ninth Sphere. The Son of Man is born of Water and Fire. When the Alchemist has completed his work in the mastery of Fire, he receives the Venustic Initiation. The betrothal of the Soul to the Lamb is the greatest festival of the Soul . That great Lord of Light enters Her. He becomes human; She becomes divine. From this divine and human mixture is born that which with so much certainty the Adorable One called "the Son of Man." The greatest triumph of supreme adoration is the birth of the Son of Man in the manger of the world. The man and woman who love each other are truly two miraculous, harmonious harps, an ecstasy of glory, that which cannot be defined because if it is defined it is disfigured. That is love. The kiss is the profound mystic consecration of two souls who adore each other, and the sexual act is the key with which we become Gods. Gods, there is God. All of you who truly love, know that God is love. To love, how beautiful it is to love. Love is nourished with love; only with love are the alchemical weddings possible. Jesus, the Beloved One, reached the Venustic Initiation in the Jordan. In the moment of the baptism, Christ entered within the adorable Jesus through the pineal gland. The word was made flesh and lived amongst us, and we beheld his glory as the Father's only son full of grace and truth." —Samael Aun Weor, The Perfect Matrimony

Soul: The modern definition and usage of this word "soul" is filled with contradictions, misconceptions, and misuse. In Gnosis (the heart of all religions), the meaning is very precise. The English word comes from the Old English sawol, meaning the "spiritual and emotional part of a person."

The spiritual and emotional part of the person is related to the sephiroth Hod (emotion), Netzach (mind), Tiphereth (will; Human Soul), and Geburah (consciousness; Divine Soul). Furthermore, these sephiroth undergo stages of growth, explained as five types or levels of soul: nephesh, neshemah, ruach, chaiah, and yechidah.

In Hinduism and Buddhism, the word soul is usually related to the Sanskrit word Atman, defined as "self." Yet, this word has been misinterpreted for centuries. The teaching of the Buddha intended to explain Atman when stating that there is no "soul" in the sense of a permanent, eternally existing element beyond the body that defines a person. Samael Aun Weor uses the word soul in the way that Buddhism uses the word "body" (of which there are physical and nonphysical bodies); each, even when created and refined, is merely a vehicle, and as such is impermanent. What is eternal is what uses those bodies.

In reality, the common person does not have a "soul" yet; they have the essence or seed of the soul, which must be grown through the "second birth." As Jesus explained, "With patience ye shall possess thy souls." (Luke 21) Thus, the development of the soul is the mere beginning of the path to full development. Afterward, there are far greater works to accomplish.

The term "soul" should not be confused with "spirit," which refers to a higher aspect of the Innermost (Atman; Chesed).

In Kabbalah, the soul has five aspects, but three are introduced first:

"The soul is a trinity. It comprises three elements, viz.: (a) Neshāmāh, the rational element which is the highest phase of existence; (b) Ruach, the moral element, the seat of good and evil, the ethical qualities; (c) Nefesh, the gross side of spirit, the vital element which is en rapport with the body, and the mainspring of all the movements, instincts, and cravings of the physical life. There is a strong reflection of Platonic psychology in these three divisions or powers of the soul . More than one mediæval Jewish theologian was a Platonist, and in all probability the Zohar is a debtor to these. The three divisions of the soul are emanations from the Sefirot. The Neshāmāh, which, as has been said, is the soul in its most elevated and sublimest sense, emanates from the Sefirah of Wisdom. The Ruach, which denotes the soul in its ethical aspect, emanates from the Sefirah of Beauty. The Nefesh, which is the animal side of the soul , is an emanation from the Sefirah of Foundation, that element of divinity which comes, most of all, into contact with the material forces of earth." —*Jewish Mysticism* by J. Abelson [1913]

Tantra: Sanskrit for "continuum" or "unbroken stream." This refers first (1) to the continuum of vital energy that sustains all existence, and second (2) to the class of knowledge and practices that harnesses that vital energy, thereby transforming the practitioner. There are many schools of Tantrism, but they can be classified in three types: White, Grey and Black. Tantra has long been known in the West as Alchemy.

"In the view of Tantra, the body's vital energies are the vehicles of the mind. When the vital energies are pure and subtle, one's state of mind will be accordingly affected. By transforming these bodily energies we transform the state of consciousness." —The 14th Dalai Lama

Tarot: "Through the Gypsies the Tarot cards may be traced back to the religious symbolism of the ancient Egyptians. [...] Court de Gébelin believed the word Tarot itself to be derived from two Egyptian words, Tar, meaning "road," and Ro, meaning "royal." Thus the Tarot constitutes the royal road to wisdom. (See Le Monde Primitif.) [...] The Tarot is undoubtedly a vital element in Rosicrucian symbolism, possibly the very book of universal knowledge which the members of the order claimed to possess. The Rota Mundi is a term frequently occurring in the early manifestoes of the Fraternity of the Rose Cross. The word Rota by a rearrangement of its letters becomes Taro, the ancient name of these mysterious cards. [...] The Pythagorean numerologist will also find an important relationship to exist between the numbers on the cards and the designs accompanying the numbers. The Qabbalist will be immediately impressed by the significant sequence of the cards, and the alchemist will discover certain emblems meaningless save to one versed in the divine chemistry of transmutation and regeneration.' As the Greeks placed the letters of their alphabet--with their corresponding numbers--upon the various parts of the body of their humanly represented Logos, so the Tarot cards have an analogy not only in the parts and members of the universe but also in the divisions of the human body.. They are in fact the key to the magical constitution of man. [...] The Tarot cards must be considered (1) as separate and complete hieroglyphs, each representing a distinct principle, law, power, or element in Nature; (2) in relation to each other as the effect of one agent operating upon another; and (3) as vowels and consonants of a philosophic alphabet. The laws governing all phenomena are represented by the symbols upon the Tarot cards, whose numerical values are equal to the numerical equivalents of the phenomena. As every structure consists of certain elemental parts, so the Tarot cards represent the components of the structure of philosophy. Irrespective of the science or philosophy with which the student is working, the Tarot cards can be identified with the essential constituents of his subject, each card thus being related to a specific part according to mathematical and philosophical laws. "An imprisoned person," writes Eliphas Levi, "with no other book than the Tarot, if he knew how to use it, could in a few years acquire universal knowledge, and would be able to speak on all subjects with unequalled learning and inexhaustible eloquence." —Manly P. Hall, *The Secret Teachings of All Ages* (1928)

Tattva: (Sanskrit) "truth, fundamental principle." A reference to the essential nature of a given thing. Tattvas are the elemental forces of nature. There are numerous systems presenting varying tattvas as fundamental principles of nature. Gnosticism utilizes a primary system of five: akash (which is the elemental force of the ether), tejas (fire), vayu (air), apas (water), and prittvi (earth). Two higher tattvas are also important: adi and samadhi.

Tree of Knowledge: (Hebrew עץ הדעת טוב ורע)

"And out of the ground made the LORD God to grow every tree that is pleasant to the sight, and good for food; the tree of life also in the midst of the garden, and the tree of knowledge of good and evil." —Genesis 2:9

From the Hebrew: עץ for tree. דעת (Daath) means "knowledge." טוב means "goodness." רע means "pollution" or "impurity."

One of two trees in the Garden of Eden, the Tree of Knowledge in Hebrew is Daath, which is related to the sexual organs and the study of sexuality, known also as Alchemy / Tantra. The full name "Tree of Knowledge of Goodness and Impurity" indicates that Daath, sexual "knowledge," leads to either "goodness" or "impurity."

Valentine, Basil: An alchemical legend whose actual identity has yet to be discovered, yet is is presumed that he lived in the fifteenth century and was likely to have been a Benedictine monk. According to tradition, his name is derived from the Greek basileus, the King, and valens, powerful, thus meaning the Powerful King, the Philosopher's Stone. His legacy is immortalized in his Twelve Keys, a series of highly symbolic drawings.

Venustic Initiations: The Venustic Initiations are the Seven Serpents of Light of the First Mountain plus one more related with the Sephirah Binah. Read *The Three Mountains*.

"...the Venustic Initiation that has eight grades. The first Venustic Initiation is just the superior octave of the first initiation of fire. The second Venustic Initiation is the superior octave of the second initiation of fire. The third Venustic Initiation is the superior octave of the third initiation of fire. The fourth Venustic Initiation is the fourth superior octave of the fourth initiation of fire. The fifth Venustic Initiation is the fifth superior octave of the fifth initiation of fire; after this come the three initiations (the total is eight) that are related with the First Mountain (that is the First Mountain). In the Second Mountain one has to begin the work with the Moon, with Mercury, with Venus, with the Sun, Mars, Jupiter, Saturn, Uranus and Neptune, to then achieve Perfection in Mastery (it is the Mountain of the Resurrection), and the Third Mountain is the Ascension, to finally crystallize (in oneself) the Second and First Logos, and to receive the Inner Atomic Star." —Samael Aun Weor, The Master Key

Vital Body: (Also called Ethereal Body) The superior aspect of the physical body, composed of the energy or vital force that provides life to the physical body.

"It is written that the vital body or the foundation of organic life within each one of us has four ethers. The chemical ether and the ether of life are related with chemical processes and sexual reproduction. The chemical ether is a specific foundation for the organic chemical phenomena. The ether of life is the foundation of the reproductive and transformative sexual processes of the race. The two superior ethers, luminous and reflective, have more elevated functions. The luminous ether is related with the caloric, luminous, perceptive, etc., phenomena. The reflective ether serves as a medium of expression for willpower and imagination." —Samael Aun Weor, *The Gnostic Bible: The Pistis Sophia Unveiled*

In Tibetan Buddhism, the vital body is known as the subtle body (lus phramo).

Vulcan: The Latin or Roman name for the Greek god Hephaistos, known by the Egyptians as Ptah. A god of fire with a deep and ancient mythology, commonly remembered as the blacksmith who forges weapons for gods and heroes.

Quotes from Paracelsus: "The office of Vulcan is the separation of the good from the bad. So the Art of Vulcan, which is Alchemy, is like unto death, by which the eternal and the temporal are divided one from another. So also this art might be called the death of things." —De Morbis Metallicis, Lib. I., Tract III., c. 1. "Vulcan is an astral and not a corporal fabricator." —De Caduco Matricis, Par. VI. "The artist working in metals and other minerals transforms them into other colours, and in so doing his operation is like that of the heaven itself. For as the artist excocts by means of Vulcan, or the igneous element, so heaven performs the work of coction through the Sun. The Sun, therefore, is the Vulcan of heaven accomplishing coction in the earth." —De Icteritiis. "Vulcan is the fabricator and architect of all things, nor is his habitation in heaven only, that is, in the firmament, but equally in all the other elements." —Lib. Meteorum, c. 4. "Where the three prime principles are wanting, there also the igneous essence is absent. The Igneous Vulcan is nothing else but Sulphur, Sal Nitrum, and Mercury." —Ibid., c.5.

White Lodge or Brotherhood: That ancient collection of pure souls who maintain the highest and most sacred of sciences: White Magic or White Tantra. It is called White due to its purity and cleanliness. This "Brotherhood" or "Lodge" includes human beings of the highest order from every race, culture, creed and religion, and of both sexes.

Yoga: (Sanskrit) "union." Similar to the Latin "religare," the root of the word "religion." In Tibetan, it is "rnal-'byor" which means "union with the fundamental nature of reality."

"The word YOGA comes from the root Yuj which means to join, and in its spiritual sense, it is that process by which the human spirit is brought into near and conscious communion with, or is merged in, the Divine Spirit, according as the nature of the human spirit is held to be separate from (Dvaita, Visishtadvaita) or one with (Advaita) the Divine Spirit." —Swami Sivananda, *Kundalini Yoga*

"Patanjali defines Yoga as the suspension of all the functions of the mind. As such, any book on Yoga, which does not deal with these three aspects of the subject, viz., mind, its functions and the method of suspending them, can he safely laid aside as unreliable and incomplete." —Swami Sivananda, *Practical Lessons In Yoga*

"The word yoga means in general to join one's mind with an actual fact..." —The 14th Dalai Lama

"The soul aspires for the union with his Innermost, and the Innermost aspires for the union with his Glorian." —Samael Aun Weor, *The Revolution of Beelzebub*

"All of the seven schools of Yoga are within Gnosis, yet they are in a synthesized and absolutely practical way. There is Tantric Hatha Yoga in the practices of the Maithuna (Sexual Magic). There is practical Raja Yoga in the work with the chakras. There is Gnana Yoga in our practices and mental disciplines which we have cultivated in secrecy for millions of years. We have Bhakti Yoga in our prayers and Rituals. We have Laya Yoga in our meditation and respiratory exercises. Samadhi exists in our practices with the Maithuna and during our deep meditations. We live the path of Karma Yoga in our upright actions, in our upright thoughts, in our upright feelings, etc." —Samael Aun Weor, *The Revolution of Beelzebub*

"The Yoga that we require today is actually ancient Gnostic Christian Yoga, which absolutely rejects the idea of Hatha Yoga. We do not recommend Hatha Yoga simply because, spiritually speaking, the acrobatics of this discipline are fruitless; they should be left to the acrobats of the circus." — Samael Aun Weor, *The Yellow Book*

"Yoga has been taught very badly in the Western World. Multitudes of pseudo-sapient Yogis have spread the false belief that the true Yogi must be an infrasexual (an enemy of sex). Some of these false yogis have never even visited India; they are infrasexual pseudo-yogis. These ignoramuses believe that they are going to achieve in-depth realization only with the yogic exercises, such as asanas, pranayamas, etc. Not only do they have such false beliefs, but what is worse is that they propagate them; thus, they misguide many people away from the difficult, straight, and narrow door that leads unto the light. No authentically Initiated Yogi from India would ever think that he could achieve his inner self-realization with pranayamas or asanas, etc. Any legitimate Yogi from India knows very well that such yogic exercises are only co-assistants that are very useful for their health and for the development of their powers, etc. Only the Westerners and pseudo-yogis have within their minds the belief that they can achieve Self-realization with such exercises.Sexual Magic is practiced very secretly within the Ashrams of India. Any True Yogi Initiate from India works with the Arcanum A.Z.F. This is taught by the Great Yogis from India that have visited the Western world, and if it has not been taught by these great, Initiated Hindustani Yogis, if it has not been published in their books of Yoga, it was in order to avoid scandals. You can be absolutely sure that the Yogis who do not practice Sexual Magic will never achieve birth in the Superior Worlds. Thus, whosoever affirms the contrary is a liar, an impostor." —Samael Aun Weor, *Alchemy and Kabbalah in the Tarot*

Yogi: (Sanskrit) male yoga practitioner.

Yogini: (Sanskrit) female yoga practitioner.

Zohar: "The Sepher ha Zohar presumably was written by Simeon ben Jochai, a disciple of Akiba. Rabbi Simeon was sentenced to death about A.D. 161 by Lucius Verus, co-regent of the Emperor Marc Aurelius Antoninus. He escaped with his son and, hiding in a cave, transcribed the manuscript of the Zohar with the assistance of Elias, who appeared to them at intervals. Simeon was twelve years in the cave, during which time he evolved the complicated symbolism of the "Greater Face" and the "Lesser Face." While discoursing with disciples Rabbi Simeon expired, and the "Lamp of Israel" was extinguished. His death and burial were accompanied by many supernatural phenomena. The legend goes on to relate that the secret doctrines of Qabbalism had been in existence since the beginning of the world, but that Rabbi Simeon was the first man permitted to reduce them to writing. Twelve hundred years later the books which he had compiled were discovered and published for the benefit of humanity by Moses de León. The probability is that Moses de León himself compiled the Zohar about A.D. 1305, drawing his material from the unwritten secrets of earlier Jewish mystics." —Manly P. Hall, *The Secret Teachings of All Ages* (1928)

Index

About the Author

His name is Hebrew סמאל און ואור, and is pronounced "sam-ayel on vay-or." You may not have heard of him, but Samael Aun Weor changed the world.

In 1950, in his first two books, he became the first person to reveal the esoteric secret hidden in all the world's great religions, and for that, accused of "healing the ill," he was put in prison. Nevertheless, he did not stop. Between 1950 and 1977 – merely twenty-seven years – not only did Samael Aun Weor write over sixty books on the most difficult subjects in the world, such as consciousness, kabbalah, physics, tantra, meditation, etc., in which he deftly exposed the singular root of all knowledge — which he called Gnosis — he simultaneously inspired millions of people across the entire span of Latin America: stretching across twenty countries and an area of more than 21,000,000 kilometers, founding schools everywhere, even in places without electricity or post offices.

During those twenty-seven years, he experienced all the extremes that humanity could give him, from adoration to death threats, and in spite of the enormous popularity of his books and lectures, he renounced an income, refused recognitions, walked away from accolades, and consistently turned away those who would worship him. He held as friends both presidents and peasants, and yet remained a mystery to all.

When one reflects on the effort and will it requires to perform even day to day tasks, it is astonishing to consider the herculean efforts required to accomplish what he did in such a short time. But, there is a reason: he was a man who knew who he was, and what he had to do. A true example of compassion and selfless service, Samael Aun Weor dedicated the whole of his life to freely helping anyone and everyone find the path out of suffering. His mission was to show all of humanity the universal source of all spiritual traditions, which he did not only through his writings and lectures, but also through his actions. He said,

"I do not want to receive visitors. Unquestionably, I am nothing more than a postman, a courier, a man that delivers a message... It would be the breaking point of silliness for you to come from your country to the capital city of Mexico with the only purpose of visiting a vulgar postman, an employee that delivered you a letter in the past... Why would you waste your money for that? Why would you visit a simple courier, a miserable postman? It is better for you to study the message, the written teachings delivered in the books...

"I have not come to form any sect, or one more belief, nor am I interested in the schools of today, or the particular beliefs of anyone! ...

"We are not interested in anyone's money, nor are we interested in monthly fees, or temples made out of brick, cement or clay, because we are conscious visitors in the cathedral of the soul and we know that wisdom is of the soul.

"Flattery tires us, praise should only belong to our Father (who is in secret and watches over us minutely).

"We are not in search of followers; all we want is for each person to follow his or her self—their own internal master, their sacred Innermost— because he is the only one who can save and glorify us.

"I do not follow anyone, therefore no one should follow me...

"We do not want any more comedies, pretenses, false mysticism, or false schools. What we want now are living realities; we want to prepare ourselves to see, hear, and touch the reality of those truths..." —Samael Aun Weor

Your book reviews matter.

Glorian Publishing is a very small non-profit organization, thus we have no money to spend on marketing and advertising. Fortunately, there is a proven way to gain the attention of readers: book reviews. Mainstream book reviewers won't review these books, but you can.

The path of liberation requires the daily balance of three active factors:

- birth of virtue
- death of vice
- sacrifice for others

Writing book reviews is a powerful way to sacrifice for others. By writing book reviews on popular websites, you help to make the books more visible to humanity, and you might help save a soul from suffering. Will you do your part to help us show these wonderful teachings to others? Take a moment today to write a review.

Donate

Glorian Publishing is a non-profit publisher dedicated to spreading the sacred universal doctrine to suffering humanity. All of our works are made possible by the kindness and generosity of sponsors. If you would like to make a tax-deductible donation, you may send it to the address below, or visit our website for other alternatives. If you would like to sponsor the publication of a book, please contact us at (844) 945-6742 or help@gnostic-teachings.org.

Glorian Publishing
PO Box 209
Clinton, CT 06413 US
Phone: (844) 945-6742
VISIT US ONLINE AT glorian.org